ROME FOR BEGINNERS

A practical guide to moving to the Eternal City

SAMANTHA CHARLTON

Rome for Beginners by Samantha Charlton

Second Edition, January 2013.

Disclaimer

The information contained within this book is for general information purposes only. While the author has taken every effort to ensure the accuracy of the information provided, no warranty or representation can be provided regarding any of the content. Any reliance you place on such information is therefore strictly at your own risk.

Throughout this book, you are able to link to other websites that are not under the control of 'Rome for Beginners'. We have no control over the nature, content and availability of those sites. The inclusion of any links does not necessarily imply a recommendation or an endorsement of the views expressed within them.

Cover design and pencil drawings by Samantha Charlton – photography from iStock photos.

www.romeforbeginners.com

***

This book is dedicated to Roma – and to all the *stranieri* who have made this city their home.

***

CONTENTS

PREFACE – WHY ROME? 4

CHAPTER ONE – BEFORE YOU GO 8

CHAPTER TWO – THE BASICS 17

CHAPTER THREE – LEARNING THE LANGUAGE............................32

CHAPTER FOUR – FINDING SOMEWHERE TO LIVE 37

CHAPTER FIVE – GETTING A JOB 52

CHAPTER SIX – TEACHING ENGLISH IN ROME 61

CHAPTER SEVEN – GETTING AROUND ROME 73

CHAPTER EIGHT – DEALING WITH CULTURE SHOCK, AND
INTEGRATING 81

CHAPTER NINE – EXPLORING ROME 87

CONCLUSION – STAYING ON?..93

APPENDIX 1...96

APPENDIX 2...97

RESOURCES 99

ABOUT THE AUTHOR...111

PREFACE – WHY ROME?

Rome is undoubtedly one of the world's great cities. She is also one of the world's greatest survivors – few cities have her ability to adapt, change and 'make do'. Yet, the beauty of Rome is also in her timelessness. Life plays out, much as it has done for centuries, in streets and *piazze* throughout the city. There are times, as you walk down one of the narrow streets in the historic centre on a hot summer afternoon, listening to the clink of cutlery and crockery from residents preparing and eating lunch, when it feels as if time has stopped.

Italy may be going through tough economic times, and those living in the capital will be among those to feel the strain the most, but Rome and her people are extremely adaptable. The city learned long ago that change is inevitable, and her inhabitants became experts in *l'arte di arrangiarsi* (the art of making do). Living in Rome will also teach you this art.

Modern Rome is a compact metropolis that often feels more like a collection of villages than a capital city. It is a layer-cake of history, a melting pot of Mediterranean culture and a smorgasbord of sensation – and delicious food! When you live in Rome, each day feels like a foray into the unexpected. Rome is never, ever boring.

Moving to Rome and setting up a life there can be daunting for a foreigner. There is so much to take in, so much to sort out. Very soon, all the practicalities can take the shine and romance off your new home. If you are not careful, you could start wondering why you moved to this noisy, frustrating and rude place!

A love affair with a new city or country is very much like a love affair with a person. Like when you become infatuated with someone you barely know, throw your entire life in with theirs, ignore any well-meaning advice from your friends, and then eventually become angry and disillusioned once you take off the rose-coloured specs – the same applies to moving to a romantic, exciting city. Initially, it all seems perfect. Your friends, family and ex-colleagues are all jealous. You spend your days in a romantic haze, searching for the perfect cappuccino, dining al fresco in sunny piazzas and buying fantastic produce at your local *rionale* market. Then, things start to bug you. The buses are too crowded, and there is never one when you are in a hurry. People knock into you on the street and don't bother to apologise. Whereas shop owners initially seemed so tolerant of your broken, stuttering Italian, you now imagine they are all sneering at you. A visit to the post office makes you understand how the phrase 'going postal' was coined, and trying to set up a bank account nearly reduces you to tears. "What's happened?" you cry, "I loved this city and I'm now starting to hate it!"

Avoiding the above situation is possible – all it takes is a bit of reality, practicality and planning. Rome has so much to offer, so much to enjoy, and *Rome for Beginners* will help you get the most out of the caput mundi, while discovering the city's gentler side. This book covers all the basics, from how to prepare for Rome before you even set foot on Italian soil, and how to get settled; to dealing with the more stressful issues like getting your paperwork sorted, finding an apartment and looking for work. There are also chapters on recognising and dealing with culture shock when it hits, and Rome's lesser-known but not-to-be-missed sights.

At this point, you may be wondering: "What makes this person qualified to lead me through the labyrinth of moving to Rome?" That's a fair question. I've had a love affair with Rome for over a decade. I moved to Rome in July 1998, when they still had the *lira*, and Luigi Scalfaro was the President of the Republic. I lived in Italy until 2005, before returning to live in Rome again in 2008.

I spent my first month in Rome wrestling with English grammar and learning how to teach, as I completed the CELTA (Cambridge Certificate in English Language Teaching to Adults) at International House in Rome. I finished my course to find myself in sweltering August heat with no job – having not realised that the summer is a bad time to look for teaching work. Luckily, I managed to find a job in Rome over the summer, teaching English in the military. With my faithful *Tuttocittà* (The Roman A to Z) in hand, I took sweltering buses to the far flung suburbs and taught English to classrooms of bored guys doing their military service. I didn't have a clue what I was doing, but my students were delighted to have a young, female teacher, and once the initial panic wore off, I even started to enjoy it.

A book like this one would have served me well in my first year in Rome.

It would have been useful to know that looking for work in August is tricky, as is trying to get a phone connected in *ferragosto* (the holiday centred around 15 August when everything in Rome closes). Back then, even those holding an EU passport (I was born in the UK), had to get a *Permesso di Soggiorno* (Permit of Stay); and it took many fruitless visits to various offices before I discovered the right place to go. As for gaining *residenza* (residence) – I was so terrified of the idea of dealing, yet again, with Italian bureaucracy, that it took me years to embark on this process. Although I did a beginner's Italian course in London before coming to Rome, I could barely manage a few words at a time. My Italian was bad enough that even the day-to-day basics of shopping for food and buying bus tickets would induce sweaty palms. Sure, I learnt fast, but when after a year and a half, I realised I was speaking a strange Italian pidgin; I enrolled in an Italian course. It took them a few months to remove the bad habits I had accumulated, but at the end of it, I was finally on my way to fluency. However, I could have saved myself a lot of stress if I had nailed my Italian early on.

I wrote this book for anyone who is planning to move, or has just moved, to Rome – and needs a practical guide to settling in with a minimum of stress. Since this is an e-book, you will find numerous hyperlinks throughout, which take you to a variety of electronic resources – some in English, and some in Italian (just copy and paste the content into Google Translate to get the gist, if you need to). I also list all of my sources in the Resources section at the back of the book, for easy reference.

Are you ready to move to the Eternal City? Let's get started!

CHAPTER ONE –
BEFORE YOU GO

"Luck is what happens when preparation meets opportunity."

~ Seneca (Roman philosopher, mid-1st century AD)

Heed Seneca's advice, and plan a little before you go. You don't need to organise every detail in an obsessive-compulsive manner, nor do you need to follow your plan with military precision – but a bit of preparation will go a long way to ensuring you aren't faced with nasty surprises, or unpleasant reality checks once you arrive in Rome. Planning is not about ruining spontaneity or turning into a worrier; it merely helps you understand what to expect, and allows you to cushion the settling-in period.

If you are reading this, you have probably made the decision to move to Rome after a wonderful holiday or study break. However, there will be some of you who have never been to Rome and want to enjoy a short period 'on holiday' before deciding whether to stay on. Whatever your situation, the following seven pieces of advice will make moving easier.

1. Choose the time of year wisely

Depending on your plans, the time of year you arrive in Rome matters.

- If you are planning on a few months break before looking for work as an English Language teacher, then arriving in June, or the beginning of December is ideal. September/October and January/February are the two best periods for looking for work as an English Language teacher.

- If you are hoping to work in tourism then you need to make sure you are in Rome during the spring (April/May) at the latest.

- If you are hoping to look for a job in administration or business, you're better off arriving in August, enjoying the tail-end of the summer, and then beginning your job hunt in mid-September.

- Note that Rome is very quiet in August – so don't expect to get much done during this month. Up until recently, the city would shut down completely during August as everyone headed for the mountains or sea. These days, many people remain in Rome for work over the summer, and there's a lot more going on – including the *estate romana* (Roman Summer) festivities. Nonetheless, many public offices and private companies will be closed.

- If you are planning on studying for up to six months upon your arrival then you should take into account that starting a three-month intensive language course in June will mean that you will be studying in 40 C (104 F). Many find it difficult to concentrate in the heat!

2. Learn some Italian before you go

This might seem elementary, but you would be amazed how many English-speaking foreigners move to Italy without more than ten words of Italian – and then complain about how hard life is!

Like it or not, the whole world does not speak English. Making an effort to get a survival Italian course under your belt before leaving will make an enormous difference to the ease with which you settle in Rome.

If you have never learnt one of the Latin languages before, you might find wrestling with masculine and feminine nouns and conjugating verbs a bit of a challenge – but when you get bogged down in grammar remember: The point of language is to be able to communicate. You will make many mistakes in the beginning – but as long as you make yourself understood – who cares? Being a perfectionist will not help you learn a language. Throw yourself in, speak Italian with passion and let go of the need to know 'why' things work the way they do. Accept Italian without trying to dissect it and you will progress quickly.

Most cities worldwide have Italian language evening classes, and failing that, there are plenty of distance and online courses. Start learning Italian at least six months before your departure – earlier if possible – and try out your newfound language skills on the internet by browsing the websites of two of Rome's major papers:

La Repubblica
www.repubblica.it/

Il Messaggero
www.ilmessaggero.it/

Remember that becoming fluent in, and mastering a language takes patience, dedication and time. This brings me to the third piece of advice…

3. Be prepared to feel stupid most of the time

This is not meant to insult your intelligence – only to warn you that you are about to embark on a massive learning curve. Be prepared not to understand basic language and cultural differences, to stand bemused while everyone laughs at a simple joke that you did not understand a word of, and to get a knotted stomach at the thought of using your newly acquired Italian on the phone.

The thing about language is that – unfairly – others often equate our ability to communicate with our level of intelligence. It is for this reason that we end up feeling stupid when we stumble and bumble over a sentence that a three-year old Italian child would handle with ease.

Ironically, the cleverer you are, and the easier you find communicating in your own language, the harder it might be for you in Rome, as you struggle to master *Italiano*. One's ego does not take well to blank stares when you have just asked for a bus ticket, nor to the shop assistant responding in English when you asked, in your best Italian, for a panino with ham and cheese!

So, before you get on the plane, take a large bite of humble pie, tell yourself to lighten up and relax a little, and remind yourself that you are going back to school. This time, Rome will be your teacher!

4. Organise your first few weeks' accommodation in advance

Organising a place to stay in advance will make your move a lot less stressful. Just the knowledge that you have a room booked for a few weeks, while you orientate yourself, will make you feel as though you already have a 'home' in Rome.

A good way to organise yourself is to enrol for a one-month language course that starts a day or two after your arrival. You should be able to organise accommodation through the school (please see <u>Chapter Three – Learning the language</u>), and they usually let you move in one or two days before the course start date.

If you decide not to go down this route, the type and quality of accommodation you go for will depend on your budget. I am assuming that most readers won't be splurging, so the two suggestions below offer low-cost options:

- Venere.com is an Italian website (you can select English) that has a wealth of accommodation all over Italy (and Europe). Just select Rome. If you are looking for a two-star pensione (a small, family-run hotel) – you can filter your search by price. Venere is generally a reliable source of accommodation, although occasionally, scammers do try their luck here. The way to recognise a scam is a 'too good to be true' price. If you do have the bad luck to stumble upon one of these – please let Venere know: www.venere.com

- Wanted in Rome is an English-language publication that has a wealth of information on jobs, housing and events in Rome. Their short-lets page has a number of options for those wanting to rent a cheap apartment or room short-term: www.wantedinrome.com/

5. Plan your finances

A common error (and one that I have repeatedly made!) is moving to a new city without enough cash. Money, and struggling to survive financially, is one of life's great stressors. Believe me – because I have lived it – trying to make a life for yourself in Rome, while having nightmares about how you are going to afford groceries this week, will quickly sap all the enjoyment out of life.

I know you won't want to hear this – but it is better to put your departure date off another six months and save like a miser, than to

arrive in Rome with pathetic savings that disappear within the first
month!

That said – how much money is enough?

A tricky question… but assuming you are travelling on a budget, you
should make sure that you have the following:

- Enough money to survive for at least three months without
  working

- An 'emergency' fund that would see you through another
  three months if you struggle to find work

- An 'extreme' emergency fund – enough money to buy a
  ticket home if you really get into dire straits (let's hope this
  never occurs – still the peace of mind is well worth it).

Working out how much you will actually spend per month is
difficult, as it will depend on how much you are spending on
accommodation. However, if you are living on a reasonably strict
budget (the odd pizza out, day-trips at the weekend, sightseeing
expenses and a morning cappuccino at the bar) your monthly
expenses will range from 1,200 to 2,000 Euros.

So, you have the money – what's the best way to bring it with you to
Rome?

- Many banks now have prepaid travel money cards. You can
  buy euros, load them onto your card, and use your card at any
  Bancomat (cash machine) in Rome – without incurring
  currency conversion or bank fees.

- Alternatively you can use your credit or debit card – but
  these will incur fees (check with your bank to find out how
  much).

- Bring around 200 euros with you in cash – but be wary about carrying around large sums of cash on your person. Rome is a pickpocket's paradise!

- Don't bother with traveller's cheques – they are just a pain these days.

- Once you are living in Rome you will need a better solution than the above, short-term, methods. Chapter Two – The Basics, provides more information on this subject.

6. Make sure you have the right documentation

Apart from the obvious of having a valid passport, make sure you are able to live and work in Italy.

- All holders of European Union passports can live and work in Italy **without** the need to obtain a permit (*Permesso di Soggiorno* – Permit of Stay)

- EU passport holders (who are registered with another EU country's healthcare system) should get a S1 form and a European Health Insurance Card (EHIC) from their local healthcare provider (please see Chapter Two – The Basics) before leaving home.

- Holders of US, Canadian, Australian and New Zealand passports do not need a visa to enter Italy, but they can only stay in Italy for periods up to three-months, and are not permitted (without the necessary visa) to work during their stay.

- Find out if you need a visa to gain entry to Italy (there are some nationalities that, due to political reasons, require a visa to enter Italy):
www.esteri.it/visti/home_eng.asp

- A list of the different types of visas for residing in Italy: www.esteri.it/visti/tipologie_eng.asp

- Italy's Ministry of the Exterior has general visa guidelines which should point you in the right direction: www.esteri.it/visti/index_eng.asp

- Take a look at Anglo Info website for an overview on residency (and the various permits) in Italy: http://rome.angloinfo.com/information/moving/residency/

7. Packing 101

They have shops in Italy. This means that you do not need to pack ten bottles of your favourite shampoo – because they probably stock it in Italian supermarkets! The old adage of taking half of what you initially intended to pack, and twice the money, is as true as ever. Here are some packing tips that work for me:

- Take just one suitcase, or large travel pack, and one carry-on.

- Be ruthless. I know it can be comforting to take your favourite books – but they will weigh down your luggage and you may never open them. Box your precious possessions up so that they can be mailed out to Rome if you decide to settle there long-term.

- When it comes to clothes – only take your winners (this means the clothes you love, that mix and match well, fit well and make you feel great when wearing them).

- Avoid bringing piles of shoes – Italy is a shoe-shopper's paradise, so limit yourself to a couple of pairs and buy once you're in Rome.

- If you're planning on job or house hunting (which I imagine you will be) make sure you bring at least one set of formal clothes. A nice (ironed) shirt and dress jacket will go a long way – as does a pair of well-fitting, new jeans (for men) and a pencil skirt and well-chosen accessories (for women). Turn up for apartment viewings dressed as if you were going to a job interview. This may seem like an overkill but Italians (like most people really) judge people by their dress. If you present yourself well you will be amazed at how much easier it is to get things done!

- Leave your white sneakers at home. If you love wearing trainers, buy dressy-looking black, grey or brown ones – or go Italian and buy silver or gold ones!

- A little preparation in advance, and a bit of thought about what you plan on doing during the 'settling in' period, will make sure your Roman adventure gets off to a winning start.

CHAPTER TWO – THE BASICS

You have done your 'pre-Rome' preparation: you have learnt some survival Italian, saved enough money to survive a few months without working, and booked yourself into a cheap *pensione* for the first month. You have also arrived mid-August so you have some 'holiday time' before searching for work, put the bulk of your savings on a travel card, sorted your documentation, packed wisely, and adopted the 'I'm ready for an adventure' attitude! Roma awaits!

Getting from the airport

Rome has two international airports – *Leonardo da Vinci* (more commonly known as *Fiumicino*), where all the big international flights and national airlines arrive and depart, and *Ciampino*, used for charter flights and bucket airlines. If you are coming from outside of Europe you are likely to arrive at *Fiumicino*, and if you are catching EasyJet or Ryanair from the UK, *Ciampino* will be your point of touch-down.

Neither airport is particularly slick or modern but, unlike Heathrow, Charles de Gaulle or LAX, you won't feel like an insignificant bug scurrying for the exit. Getting to the centre from either airport is easy.

Fiumicino

Train: Follow the 'Treni' signs in the main Arrivals hall, up two fights of escalators, and you will find the train station on your right. You can buy tickets at:

- The main ticket windows (although if you have an early morning arrival, these might not be open)
- The automatic machines (watch out for pickpockets!)
- The Tabacchio (tobacconist's).

Two trains take you into the centre of Rome:

1. The Leonardo Express (a contradiction in terms really), which goes to Rome's main train station – Roma Termini – and does not stop en route.
2. The metropolitan train (*treno metropolitana*) that stops everywhere, and is the one you will need if you are staying anywhere near Trastevere, Ostiense, Tuscolana or Tiburtina (be careful of thieves on this route).

For detailed information from Trenitalia on the Leonardo Express and the Metropolitan Train from Fiumicino to Rome, please see hyperlink 15 in the Resources section:

When asking for a one-way ticket for the Metropolitan service, you will need to specify which station you are getting off at (refer to map link above). Say:

Un biglietto solo andata per Roma (insert name of station here) *per favore.*

Remember to stamp your ticket in one of the orange or yellow machines on the platform BEFORE you get on the train. Failure to do so will result in a fine.

The train ride should take around 30 minutes.

Taxi: There is a taxi rank right outside the Arrivals terminal. Only catch one of the taxis queued up here – and ignore the touts who shout "taxi!" as you come out of Arrivals (these guys will rip you off).

A one-way journey into the centre of Rome should cost approximately 50 Euros. Always check first:

Quanto costa per andare al centro di Roma?
How much to go to the centre of Rome?

They might ask you to specify where in the centre of Rome (Dove?). Just give them the street name and number, as well as the name of the hotel.

They should respond "cinquanta" (fifty) or at the most "sessanta" (sixty).

Note: Learn your Italian numbers before you go and life will be a lot easier!

Ciampino

Ciampino used to be a real pain in the neck to travel to and from – although these days it is easy!

There is a scheduled COTRAL (the blue regional buses) line but it is inconvenient and slow.

The best option is to take one of the Terravision coaches. These are cheap, regular, reliable, and will drop you off on Via Marsala, just outside Termini Station. The bus ride takes around 40 minutes.

For the Rome Ciampino page of the Terravision website, please see hyperlink 16 in the Resources section.

Your airline might offer you a coach ticket to the centre of Rome – which you can purchase on-board. These are usually a bit more expensive than Terravision but convenient.

Orientation

You have arrived – checked in to your accommodation and slept off your jet lag. Now it is time to get your bearings. No matter what time of year, Rome is an assault on the senses. However, if you arrive in the summer, you will also have to adjust to the heat. Take things slowly, do your sightseeing during the coolest parts of the day and take an afternoon nap. Drink lots of water, especially the sparkling kind (which is high in the minerals that you will be sweating out). Rome's *nasoni* (literally, 'big noses' – the fire-hydrant shaped water fountains all over the city), provide cool, delicious drinking water. Rome is the only city in Italy to have *nasoni*, and in hot weather they are invaluable. The water is perfectly safe to drink so feel free to refill your water bottle at these fountains as you explore the city.

Do not be surprised if you feel a bit 'zombie-like' for the first couple of days – it will wear off!

One of the things you will need before striking out on your own is an idea of how the public transport system works, and a good map. You should be able to pick up a tourist map at a tourist information kiosk, or at your hotel.

The Mappery has a good map of central Rome to get you started: www.mappery.com/Rome-Tourist-Map

A fantastic (and accurate) guide that all Romans swear by is *Tuttocittà*. Although the printed version is many a newcomer's bible, the online maps are brilliant. Plus, if you are looking for how to get to a specific street, just type the address into the search field and hit 'trova' (find): www.tuttocitta.it/mappa/roma

Something to keep in mind as you hit the streets and get to grips with Rome's public transport network is that, by law, everyone living in Italy has to carry an identity card or passport on them at all times. Since, carrying around your passport in Rome is a risky business, I recommend carrying a photocopy around in your wallet instead. That way, if stopped by the police, you have something to hand.

Rome's public transport network is comprehensive and cheap. However, it is overburdened so if you can manage it, try to avoid using the metro or buses at rush hour (between 7.30am and 10am and between 5pm and 8.30pm – yes Rome's rush-hours are long!).

ATAC run Rome's bus and metro network and their website gives you a comprehensive map of their entire network: www.atac.roma.it/index.asp?lingua=ENG

(Note: At the time of writing, the new Line C is still a year away from completion)

ATAC raised their tariffs (for the first time in years) in May 2012 – although it is still a good deal. Here is a selection of the most useful tickets (and current prices):

- BIT (€ 1.50): valid for 100 minutes from when you stamp the ticket (this is the classic ticket that you will purchase).
- BIG (€ 6.00): a day ticket, valid for 24 hours from when you stamp it – for an unlimited number of trips within Rome's city limits.
- BTI (€ 16.50): a three-day ticket, valid until midnight of the third day after you stamp it. Like the BIG, this ticket is valid for an unlimited number of trips within Rome's city limits.
- CIS (€ 24.00): a seven-day ticket, valid until midnight of the seventh day after you stamp it. Like the BIG and the BTI, this ticket is valid for an unlimited number of trips within Rome's city limits.

A great deal, especially if you are considering using the public transport long term, is the monthly pass (*abbonamento mensile*). This costs 35 Euros and is valid for the calendar month. Like the above tickets, you can use it for unlimited trips within Rome's city limits.

You can buy bus/metro tickets from newsagents, tobacconists and Termini Station. If you wish to buy a single ticket, say:

Buongiorno/Buonasera, un biglietto per l'autobus/per la metro per favore?

If you want to buy a monthly pass, say:

Vorrei un'abbonamento mensile per (insert month here) *per favore.*

Finally, remember to *timbrare* (stamp) your ticket! This will not seem obvious at first, but once you have received a *multa* (fine) you won't forget about doing this. You insert your ticket into little orange or yellow machines inside buses and at the Metro turnstiles, so that they can print the date and time; failure to do so means your ticket is still 'live', so you could use it again. The same rule applies for catching a train, only this time you stamp your ticket BEFORE you get on. You will see many machines on the platform.

Now you have a bus pass and a good map in hand, there should be no stopping you. However, the best way to get orientated in Rome is to walk. Put on good walking shoes, get out your street map and begin your voyage of discovery!

Getting into a Roman Rhythm

One of the first things a newcomer from an English-speaking country notices is how very different the daily rhythm of life is in Rome. Italians are early risers, especially the elderly. Markets and coffee bars open in early dawn, and at the height of the summer, it is common to see old women out with their shopping bags at 6am!

Nothing much happens during the afternoon (1.30pm-4pm) so use this quiet time to do your supermarket shopping, take a nap, or read a book. Shops re-open at around 4pm and do not close until 8pm, giving you plenty of time to get a bit of retail therapy in. Locals eat around 8.30-9pm – and then the evening stretches on after that. On a summer's evening out in Rome, it really is possible to lose sense of time.

Here are some tips for developing a Roman Rhythm:

- Stroll, saunter, wander – don't frog-march your way around Rome. Look at the way locals walk. They take in their surroundings and stroll as if they have all the time in the world. Getting from A to B in record time on foot (this does not count for scooters!) does not win you any prizes here.

- When queuing for anything – be patient, and persistent! I know it is easier said than done, but standing there seething for half an hour won't help. Once you reach the head of the queue, don't let some harassed clerk intimidate you so that you don't end up getting the information you came for! Take a deep breath and keep asking questions (draw pictures if you have to!), until you have all the information you need.

- Food is a passion in Italy. Italians cherish their daily eating rituals, and if you do the same you will soon feel part of things. Stand up in your local bar for a *cappuccino* and *cornetto* at breakfast and, if you have access to a kitchen, make sure you shop every couple of days for fresh food. Romans often consume a sit-down lunch, rather than a sandwich on the run, although for most Romans, the evening meal is now the main meal of the day.

- Pizza and pasta are Italian favourites but if your diet consists entirely of these two foodstuffs you will soon start to resemble a *calzone*! Even though many Italians eat pasta every day, they do not scoff down huge bowls of it, and vegetables or salad always follow the pasta course. Get into the habit of including fresh fruit and vegetables with every meal.

- When shopping at your local supermarket, pay attention to what other shoppers are doing. For example, you must put on a pair of plastic disposable gloves if you are helping yourself to fruit and vegetables; and weigh and label them yourself. The deli and bakery counters are always crowded so make sure you get yourself a number and keep an eye on the electronic display so you don't miss your turn!

- Once you start meeting locals, and get invited to someone's home for dinner, you will experience one of the joys of living in Italy. Notice how informal and warm the whole occasion is; how you are involved in the preparation – and how the meal nearly always consists of an *antipasto* (starter), *primo* (first course of pasta or risotto), and *secondo* (fish or meat served with vegetables). *Dolce* (dessert) is usually small and sweet (often just a couple of tiny pastries picked up from the local bakery). The meal concludes with an espresso and/or a shot of *amaro, limoncello* or *grappa.*

- Start to feel like a local by finding a coffee bar you love and making it 'your bar'. Soon the barista will be greeting you with a robust: "Ciao!" Go to the same cashier in the supermarket, the same market stalls when buying fruit and vegetables, and the same butcher or fishmonger. By establishing local contact and acquaintances, you will feel part of Rome's daily life in no time at all!

Getting the basics sorted – budgeting, tax code, permit of stay, telephones & internet access, healthcare and basic banking

Budgeting

In <u>Chapter One – Before you go</u> I estimate that your monthly expenses (including accommodation) should range between 1,200 and 2000 Euros. This of course, is dependent on the type of accommodation you go for, whether or not you are sharing the costs, and how many additional expenses you have.

Like many newcomers to Rome, I imagine you will initially be on a tight budget – especially if you have not yet found work. Here are some tips that will help your Euros go a little further:

- do the bulk of your supermarket shopping at discount supermarkets and local markets, outside the centre if possible. Shop where the locals do.

- buy a monthly travel pass for the public transport – this only costs 35 Euros. Save buying a car or scooter till later (you'll need to get *residenza* for this anyway – see <u>Chapter Four – Finding somewhere to live</u>).

- visit Rome's flea markets for clothing – especially summer clothing, costume jewellery and sandals – there are some real bargains to be found!

- if you're running low on cash but want to be able to enjoy a meal out – make sure you go out for an *aperativo*. Typically a northern custom, the *aperativo* is a before-dinner drink, accompanied by a selection of tasty bar snacks. Some bars put on a fantastic spread. For the cost of one or two beers or wines you can have a light meal (try not to be too greedy). The *tavola calda* is another cheap meal option. Literally 'hot table', these establishments serve the food 'canteen-style' – and are a lot cheaper than restaurants.

- if the cost of hiring a deckchair and beach umbrella at any of the beach resorts near Rome is a bit steep for your budget, remember that every stretch of beach has a 'free' area.

- when eating out, avoid the historic centre or Vatican area. Just sitting down for a glass of wine outside a bar or restaurant in these areas could blow your weekly budget. These bars often bring 'extras' to your table unasked, e.g. water, and then charge you for them!

Il Codice Fiscale – Tax Code

Although you certainly do not want to spend your first weeks in Rome wrestling with Italian bureaucracy, there are a couple of things worth sorting as soon as you get settled. The first of these is a tax code – *il codice fiscale*. Without this handy little number, it is impossible to get simple things done, like opening a bank account or getting paid.

Like most countries, Italy wants its residents to pay tax – hence getting a *codice fiscale* is a lot easier than many other bureaucratic feats!

You get a *codice fiscale* from the Income Agency (*Agenzia delle Entrate*) located on Via Ippolito Nievo, 36.

When you turn up at the Income Agency make sure you bring your:

- valid passport (European Union citizens) and proof of address where the agency can send your new card – this could be a letter sent to you from your landlord, or language school; or failing this, a piece of paper with the address typed out.

- valid passport with relevant visa/s (non-European Union citizens), a valid Permit of Stay (*Permesso di Soggiorno* – see notes below about this), proof of address, and an identity card or birth certificate from your country of origin.

Once you queue at the *sportello* (window) and hand-over your details, you will be given a printout of your new *codice fiscale*. Keep this safe and use it until your plastic card arrives by post.

Permesso di Soggiorno – Permit of Stay

This used to be a big head-ache for everyone – EU or non-EU citizens alike. Now, only non-EU passport-holders require them.

If you have a European Union passport you no longer require a *Permesso di Soggiorno*. The following applies to non-EU passport holders only.

The Italian state has streamlined (although this implies that it makes sense, which it does not) the whole process. You used to have to queue at the police headquarters, fight your way through the crowds, endure humiliation at the desk and fight your way back again days or weeks later to pick up your document. Now, the process works as follows:

1. You go to the *Sportello del Cittadino* (Citizens' Window/Desk) at one of the big post offices (San Silvestro, Bologna or Ostiense) and request an application packet for a *Permesso di Soggiorno ("Posso prendere il pachetto per il permesso di soggiorno?"*) Take it away and spend a couple of days filling it in (no really, it is huge, complicated and requires a good dictionary).

2. Return to the same post office with the completed form, all the documentation you require, special adhesive stamps (*marca da bollo* which you buy from tobacconists), passport

photos and the fee (don't forget to ask about this when you pick up the form).

3. If you have filled the form in correctly and provided everything required, the post office will process your request, hand you a confirmation slip and send you on your way.

4. A month or two later you will receive a text, letter or email from the police, informing you of the date and time of your appointment – and the location. You would like to think that this is the last step, but no – you will probably have to trek back and forth a few times (and to different police stations), as you will also need to get your hand-print digitally scanned.

For handy blogs containing more information on the Permit of Stay process, please visit hyperlinks 21 & 22 in the Resources section

Telephones & Internet Access

These days, there is really no need to go through the rigmarole of getting a landline installed. Italians love their mobile phones (*cellulare* or *telefonino*), and rates for calling and texting (*mandare un SMS*) are generally very competitive.

Getting set up for a mobile phone is very easy – especially if you bring your mobile from home. All you need to buy is a *Carta SIM* (SIM card) from any mobile telephone outlet (Vodafone, TIM – *Telecom Italia Mobile*, Tre and Wind are the main providers). Just bring in your passport (and your *codice fiscale* if you have one). To make life easier, just get 'pay as you go' (*ricaricabile*), rather than a prepaid plan (which you often need *residenza* for – please see Chapter Four: Finding somewhere to live). You can buy top-ups for your phone at all *tabacchi* (tobacconist shops) – just say: *Una ricarica di venti euro/cinquanta euro per Vodafone/TIM/Tre/Wind per favore*. The audio instructions are in Italian so you may need to get someone to help you top up your phone initially.

Even without a landline, there are a couple of options for getting internet access. The first option is that you can log on to one of the *internet gratuito senza fili* (free WiFi hotspots) within Rome. All you need is an Italian mobile phone number to log on to the network.

For an informative blog with detailed information on WiFi, how to access it, and a map of free WiFi hotspots in Rome, please visit hyperlink 19 in the Resources section.

Alternatively, you can buy an Internet Key from one of the mobile phone providers (prices are pretty reasonable these days), which will give you WiFi access. Just plug the Internet Key into your laptop or tablet – and away you go!

Healthcare in Rome

The healthcare system in Italy is publically funded; so those registered with the *servizio sanitario nazionale* (SSN) get free or heavily subsidised healthcare and medicines. The quality of treatment varies hugely from hospital to hospital.

To register for the SSN you will need *residenza* (please see Chapter Four – Finding somewhere to live). If you are an EU citizen, and are registered with the national health in your country, make sure to fill in a S1 form and get yourself a European Health Insurance Card (EHIC) before your arrival in Rome. This is not health insurance, but, instead, will entitle you to use the public health system without the need to gain *residenza* first. Visit the European Commission's website for more information on the S1 form and the EHIC (hyperlink 24 in the Resources section).

If you don't have *residenza,* or aren't eligible for an EHIC, then you will need to use private healthcare while in Rome. Don't despair – the private healthcare is generally of a high standard and not prohibitively expensive. Remember that if you have an accident or fall ill suddenly, the emergency department (*pronto soccorso*) of all public hospitals will accept you and provide first response treatment free. When looking for a private doctor your best source of information will always be your local pharmacy – *farmacia*. Italian pharmacists are highly knowledgeable and they will have a listing of all the public and private doctors in the area. If you want to be really sure you have adequate healthcare cover, it's worth taking out private health insurance, either at home or once you arrive in Rome.

Basic Banking

Italian banks are, for the most part, inefficient and inconvenient – with huge monthly fees to boot. If you could avoid embroiling yourself with one, you would be doing yourself a huge favour; however, you will need to get one eventually.

As you are likely to have bank accounts and a credit card from home – keep these for most of your initial banking and get yourself a Postpay card from the *Poste Italiane* (Italian Post). However, longer term (and if you want to get *residenza* – please see Chapter Four – Finding somewhere to live) you will need an actual bank account.

La carta Postpay

The Postpay card (you just need the standard one), costs 5 Euros and is issued while you wait at the post office. You will need your *codice fiscale* and passport. Your Postpay card 'looks' like a Visa debit card, but is just a pre-paid card. You do not need a bank account to set one up, and there are no monthly fees. You can transfer money into it using Paypal, draw money out from *Bancomat* (money machines) and buy goods online like a regular debit card. You can also use it overseas. I've found these cards fantastic and simple to use – in a country where too much is complicated!

Eventually, you may need to open a bank account (for receiving your wages and if you are paying rent via direct credit). Once again, *Poste Italiane* is worth trying – ask about one of their *Bancoposta* options.

If you do decide to open a bank account in Italy, bring your work contract with you, and/or a letter from your employer, plus a payslip to prove that you are earning – and dress well! Once you find a job, many employers are happy to accompany you to the bank to put in a good word for you.

For more information on the Postpay card and Bancoposta account (in Italian), please see hyperlinks 25-26 in the Resources section.

Transferring money

One of the first things you will need to figure out is how to transfer funds, easily and cheaply from your home bank accounts to your new Postpay or bank account in Rome.

There are a few options out there, but the best I have discovered is Paypal.

It is easy – you set up an account with www.paypal.com – and load your home cheque account on to it. Then set up another account with www.paypal.it and load your Postpay or Italian bank account number on to it. You will need a separate email addresses for each account – and then you can send money to yourself, both ways, with a minimum of fees and hassle. Usually, transfers take two to five working days, but are still much faster (and cheaper) than making international transfers through your bank.

CHAPTER THREE – LEARNING THE LANGUAGE

I touched on learning Italian in Chapter One, but my advice still bears repeating: learn some Italian before you leave and you will find settling in much easier. You don't need to get up to conversational level, but if you can buy food and bus tickets, order a meal, ask for directions (and understand the answer!), introduce yourself and tell people a little about where you are from; the language barrier will be considerably lowered.

Once you arrive in Rome, it is a good idea to book yourself into a language course. You may decide to spend your first month (or longer) studying full-time – and this is a clever move. For peace of mind, organise the course before your departure, plus get your accommodation sorted too. Many language schools will assist with accommodation, from home-stays with local families, to flat-shares with other students, or your own studio apartment (obviously, the most expensive option).

Embarking on an Italian language course is a great way to start your Roman adventure. It gives you a 'project' while buying you time before looking for work. You also have the chance to make some friends, even if they are probably going to be other foreigners, which will help you feel settled.

Rome has plenty of Italian language schools. Here is a short list (though not exhaustive):

DILIT – International House:
www.dilit.it/

Torre di Babele – Italian Language School:
www.torredibabele.com/

Scuola Leonardo Da Vinci:
www.scuolaleonardo.com/Italian-language-school-Rome.html

Istituto Dante Alighieri:
www.languageinitaly.com/EN/dante_alighieri.php

If becoming a full-time student for a month or two does not appeal, the above schools all run evening classes for those who have to work during the day.

If you are serious about getting fluent in Italian, then a course (or private tuition) while living in Rome is highly recommended. And if you plan on getting an office job, or any job where you will be competing against native Italian speakers, I also recommend you consider doing a preparatory course for, and sitting, one of the CILS (*Certificazione di Italiano come Lingua Straniera*) exams.

The CILS exam is held twice a year in June and December. This certificate is a title of proficiency in the Italian language and is recognised by the Italian Ministry of Foreign Affairs. There are basically six levels of CILS, A1 being the most basic and C2 the most advanced.

Torre di Babele provides a useful page of information on the CILS (including levels, exam dates, preparatory courses and prices).

For more information on the CILS (*Certificazione di Italiano come Lingua Straniera*), please visit hyperlink 33 in the Resources section.

Now that you are actually in Rome, doing a language course and surrounded by Italian, you will expect your Italian improve rapidly – and it will. However, the path to mastery and fluency of a language requires time, patience and persistence. I have spent many years as a language teacher (both English and Italian), and began learning Italian in my early twenties. It took me nearly two years to become fluent (largely due to slackness on my part!) but I learnt some valuable lessons about learning Italian along the way. Here are some tips I wish someone had given me!

- Enrol in a course – even a part-time one will work magic – otherwise you have the odious task of forcing yourself to study on your own. A few heroic individuals do manage to master a language through books, DVDs and CDs – and a lot of self-discipline – but most of us need some help!

- Watch Italian TV! I know it is rubbish, and I know most of it will seem incomprehensible at first, but your vocabulary and comprehension will improve out-of-sight. There are a few good programmes out there. Try watching the *Telegiornale* (TV news) and look out for any new mini-series – these are usually light-hearted and great for your Italian. One of my favourite travel and documentary programmes is *Alle Falde del Kilimangiaro*: www.allefaldedelkilimangiaro.rai.it

- Personalise your notes. If you are doing a course you will receive a course book and notes – make these your own. Write your own notes, vocabulary-lists and verb tables; doing so will help you retain information.

- Don't let set-backs get you down. Accept that people will stare at you blankly at times, that others will respond in English, and some might make rude comments about your Italian (most people are lovely but there are always a few exceptions). Take all of this in your stride and don't let it destroy your sense of self-worth, or let it make you bitter against Italians. And remember, any foreigner, in any country, who is learning the native language, goes through this – you are not alone!

- Struggling to learn a new language does not make you stupid! At the risk of over-simplifying the entire process, you should know that there are studies which show that intelligence and the ability to acquire a new language, do not necessarily go together. Actually, the cleverer you are the more your ability to 'make sense' of things and analyse, might trip you up. Many think that children learn languages easily because their minds are developing and thus like 'sponges' but it is more than that. I believe that children also learn quickly because they 'accept' a new language without trying to fit it into neat boxes in their minds. How can this help you? By accepting that in the early stages of learning Italian, you will have a lot of information that you cannot possibly make sense of. Accept this and move forward anyway! You do not need to know 'why' something is, in order to use it. Perfectionism in the early stages of language learning is counter-productive. There will be plenty of time for that once you have mastered the language!

- Keep a sense of humour. Frankly, I said some ridiculous things while learning Italian – and I said them earnestly, thinking I was saying something else entirely. You will make mistakes; you will mix up your masculine and feminine nouns and tell Italians something ridiculous, nuts or obscene without realising it. Many a foreigner has told a dinner table of Italians that "This fig is good!" and wonders why everyone's jaw drops in shock – or announces that "This apricot jam doesn't have any preservatives," and then wonders why everyone starts giggling (go and look these two up!). It is all part of the process so laugh with them, or apologise for your unintended rudeness and move on.

- Find yourself a good self-study book – preferably one that highlights communicative, everyday language, and handy situation-specific vocabulary, such as opening a bank account, registering with your local *anagrafe* (registry office), getting a *permesso di soggiorno* or applying for *residenza*. My favourite is: *Come si dice...?* by Elisa Ferri and Maria Cristina Peccianti (Giunti Demetra). While this isn't a beginner's book, it's great once you've got a bit of elementary Italian under your belt - you can buy *Come si dice...?* on Amazon (please see hyperlink 34 in the Resources section).

- Immerse yourself. Make friends with Italians as soon as you can, invite your newfound friends over for dinner, organise day-trips with them or go out for a pizza – and immerse yourself in the language. Listen to Italian music, eavesdrop on people's conversations and watch clips from Italian TV on You Tube. Embrace Italian culture, habits and lifestyle and the language will follow.

CHAPTER FOUR – FINDING SOMEWHERE TO LIVE

One of the basics for feeling 'at home' in Rome is finding yourself a 'base'. You might be lucky, and the accommodation you arranged before arriving might turn into something longer term. However, if you have been living in a *pensione* (small, family-run hotel) you will need to find a real *casa* before your savings dry up.

There are a few of things to take into consideration when house hunting.

Rent or buy?

As most of us cannot afford to buy an apartment in Rome, I will assume you are looking for rented accommodation. Buying property in Italy is another, complex subject that deserves a book of its own!

Which neighbourhood?

This is an important consideration. If you choose to live within the *centro storico* (historic centre) or within the ancient city walls (which define Rome's centre), you will pay more but be able to walk most places, and won't need to go far in the evening. Rome's historic centre is beautiful but the downside of living there is the lack of a real sense of 'neighbourhood', as many Romans cannot afford to live in the centre anymore. The centre is also very busy, full of tourists and not as friendly or as intimate as beyond the city walls. If you choose to live a bit further out, there are some beautiful suburbs that are well connected to the centre. You will need to use public transport (or a bicycle or scooter) more often, and will need to rely on night buses or taxis to get home after an evening out in the centre. The suburbs are cheaper to live in, not just for rent, but the supermarkets and shops cater for locals, rather than tourists.

If you are set on living in the centre, three areas (for me) stand out:

Trastevere – on the other side of the river (cross Ponte Garibaldi or Ponte Sisto to reach it). This quarter used to be where Rome's artisans lived and it still has a village-like feel. Trastevere (literally 'across the Tiber') has plenty of places to go in the evenings and is a gorgeous tangle of ivy-covered (and graffiti-covered) streets.

Testaccio – a grid of streets just south-west of the Aventine Hill, and a short walk along the river from the centre. Testaccio sits next to Rome's old slaughterhouse, and still retains some of its old, earthy charm. You'll find some of Rome's best *trattorie* here. Testaccio is also well linked via public transport, with plenty of trams and buses. Ostiense train station and the Metro stop *Piramide* (Line B) are also located nearby.

Monti – this is a tangle of streets between the busy triangle of Via Cavour, Via dei Fori Imperiali and Via Nazionale – and is all that remains of Rome's medieval quarter. It is a little hidden treasure in the centre of Rome and certainly worth house-hunting in if you want to live in the heart of things.

If you decide to venture out just beyond the ancient walls, there are some winners:

Porta Pia – located just outside the ancient wall's eastern gate, not far from Termini. This area is tightly packed (just off the busy Via Nomentana) with great shops, restaurants and a fantastic covered market. Porta Pia has excellent transport links and is a short walk to Villa Borghese Park.

Flaminio – located just outside the northern-most gate, behind the Flaminio (Metro A) metro and light-rail station. This area runs alongside the eastern bank of the Tiber, is close to Villa Borghese Park and characterised by its quiet streets and elegant buildings.

Prati – located on the west bank of the Tiber, not far from Rome's law-courts and the Vatican. Wide, tree-lined boulevards, lovely architecture and plenty of shops characterise this area.

San Giovanni and Rè di Roma – San Giovanni lies just outside the southern-most gate and Rè di Roma is a little further south. The Appia Nuova – a wide street crammed with shops – begins just beyond the wall and stretches south, through Piazza di Rè di Roma. There are plenty of amenities in this area and it is a short walk from the huge Appia Antica Park.

Monteverde – located up on the hill, to the west of Trastevere. Monteverde is divided into two areas: new (Monteverde Nuovo) and old (Monteverde Vecchio). It is a green neighbourhood and near the huge park, Villa Pamphili.

A little further afield there are more gems:

Piazza Bologna – located on the Metro B line (Bologna), a solid middleclass area with wide, leafy streets and Villa Torlonia (a small park). There are plenty of supermarkets, shops and coffee bars, as well as excellent transport links into the centre.

Trieste and the **Quartiere Africano** – another green, pretty and comfortable suburb (close to Villa Ada – a huge urban park), a bit further north than Piazza Bologna, so named because most of its streets use the names of Italy's former colonies: Eritrea, Somalia and Ethiopia.

Garbatella – a charming and atmospheric neighbourhood, and well-linked (just south of Ostiense train station and with its own metro stop – B Line 'Garbatella'). This quarter has its old and new parts, some great *trattorie*, and is a short walk to the Appia Antica Park.

San Lorenzo – the student district, just southeast of the city walls (around ten minutes' walk to Termini station). Tightly packed, and a little grimy and gritty, San Lorenzo is perfect for anyone who wants to spend their evenings rubbing elbows with left-wing students in the many pubs and clubs in the district. There are also some fantastic eateries in this area.

Of course, with the exception of Garbatella and San Lorenzo, you might find the above all too 'middle-class' and not 'real' enough for your taste. If this is the case, then try looking for a place to live in one of the following areas:

Casalina and **Prenestina** – these two suburbs stretch south of the wall and are densely populated with uninspiring architecture and traffic-clogged roads. There isn't a lot of green here, and rent is pretty cheap compared to elsewhere – and there does appear to be some regeneration happening in this area.

Centocelle – located further south, beyond Prenestina. This area was always one of Rome's grittiest, but it has improved of late and, due to the forthcoming opening of Rome's Metro C line, it may become more sought after in future.

Aurelia – the vast suburbs that stretch west. The Aurelia is pretty nondescript, and densely populated in places, but well linked by the Metro A line to the centre of Rome.

Montesacro and **Salario** – the vast suburbs that stretch east. Linked mostly by express buses from Termini but since the opening of the new section of the B1 line to Conca d'Oro in Montesacro, this area will no doubt become more popular – and expensive.

For a full listing of all of Rome's suburbs, with detailed descriptions of each – Wanted in Rome has a useful "Where to live" page: www.wantedinrome.com/where-to-live

Room-share, flat-share or your own place? This will all depend on your age, maturity, personality and budget. If you are young, into the student lifestyle and don't mind having zero privacy then *posto letto* (room-share) is by far the cheapest option. Depending on the area, and the quality of the building, the price for room-share can range between 150-500 Euros per month.

The next step up is a *camera* or *stanza* in a shared apartment. This is a great way to make Italian friends (provided you don't end up with a group of foreigners) and is ideal while you get settled in Rome. Often, renting your own place straight away before establishing your social network, is a sure-fire way to end up a bit lonely. The cost of a room in a shared flat ranges between 400-700 Euros per month.

A *monolocale* (studio apartment) or *mini-appartamento/bi-locale* (a one-bedroom apartment) are the only choice for those who are 'over' sharing. These cost from around 700 Euros up, per month.

Now you have an idea about where you would like to live, as well as the type of accommodation you are looking for – it is time to start looking.

Wanted in Rome is the first port of call for English-speaking foreigners. This is an online (and printed) magazine that has a wealth of information for foreigners. They have advertisements for short-lets, apartments and rooms and flat-shares. Take a look at the accommodation section of their website: www.wantedinrome.com/clas/index.php

Porta Portese is another source of accommodation (the buy-and-sell magazine of the same name as Rome's famous Sunday flea-market). Porta Portese is in Italian so it is worth getting some handy vocabulary under your belt (see vocabulary list below) before navigating your way through its *affitto* e *subaffitto* (to let and sub-let) listing – please see hyperlink 37 in the Resources section).

If Wanted in Rome and Portaportese do not bear fruit – try:

Craigslist:
www.rome.en.craigslist.it/

Bakeca:
www.roma.bakeca.it/case-0

Apartments – Handy Vocabulary (in alphabetical order)

Ampio/a - spacious
Antico – top floor/penthouse/attic apartment
Arredato/immobilato - furnished
Ben collegata – well linked (via public transport)
Delizioso/a - delightful
Fino a – up to/until
Grande - large
Grazioso/a – gracious
Il bagno/il servizio – bathroom
Il balconcino – little balcony
Il balcone – balcony
Il box – garage
Il prezzo – price
Il ripostiglio – storeroom
Il salone – lounge
Il soggiorno – living room
Il soppalco – mezzanine floor
L'angolo cottura – corner (open-plan) kitchenette
L'armadio – wardrobe
L'ascensore – lift/elevator

L'ingresso – entrance
La camera/la stanza – room/bedroom
La cameretta – small room
La cucina – kitchen
La finistra – window
La porta – door
La terrazza – terrace
Nuova costruzione – new build
Oltre – above/other
Ottima condizione – top/great condition
Panoramico – with great views
Piccolo/a - small
Posto auto – parking place
Ristrutturato – rennovated
Senza prezzo – without price

Apartment hunting and dealing with agents and landlords

No matter where you find a listing for a room or apartment, you are going to have to make that phone call:

Buongiorno/Buonasera, ho visto l'annuncio a Portaportese. E' ancora disponibile l'appartamento/la camera?
Hello, I'm calling about the ad in Portaportese. Is the apartment/room still available?

Quando posso vederlo? (for the apartment)
Quando posso vederla? (for the room)
When may I see it?

So you visit the apartment and you like it. Here are a few vital questions to ask (if the advertisement did not already make this clear):

Quant'è l'affitto?
How much is the rent?

L'affitto comprende tutte le spese?
Does the rent include all bills?

Quali sono le spese?
What bills are extra?

C'è un contratto?
Is there a contract?

Quant'è il deposito cauzionale?
How much is the deposit?

Quanto devo pagare in anticipo?
How much must I pay in advance?

Quando è disponibile l'appartamento?
When is the room/apartment available?

Non ho ancora organizzato un conto bancario. Posso pagare in contanti per ora?
I don't have a bank account yet. Can I pay cash for the moment?

In most cases the deposit is a month's rent. If you go via a real-estate agency (*agente immobiliare*) you usually have to pay a month's rent to them as a fee. Most landlords will ask for one to two months' rent up front (*in anticipo*) as well.

If you are renting a room in Rome, it is unlikely you will have to sign a contract. The person who rented the apartment initially will have the contract in their name (if they have a contract at all).

If you are renting an apartment, by law, you should have a contract. However, many landlords in Rome – in trying to avoid paying tax – try to get around this by not offering you a contract (and letting you pay cash monthly). This may seem tempting but remember if you accept this arrangement you:

- have no rights or comeback if you have problems with your landlord (e.g. the landlord refuses to pay for a plumber when your hot water cylinder stops working)

- your landlord won't like it if you try to apply for *residenza* (residence) – essential if you wish to purchase a scooter/car or sign on to the public health system (see notes below about this). The reason why they get twitchy about this is that, once you apply for residence, the police usually pay a visit to the apartment to check you actually live there. If they ask to see your contract and you don't have one – you and the landlord could be in big trouble.

If you are renting an apartment it is also likely that you will have to pay for *il condominio* (service/building charge). This can range from 50-200 Euros per month – generally, the bigger the building (and the more lifts, cleaners and porters it has), the more expensive the *condominio* is.

You will also be charged for the following:

La nettezza urbana – Rubbish collection
Il gas – Cooking gas
L'acqua – Water

Rental Contracts

There are two types of 'official' rental contracts in Italy:

- A free market contract: *contratto a libero mercato* (often known as a 4x4 – Quattro più Quattro - contract. This is for four years, and renewable for another four-year period, in which the tenant and the landlord agree the conditions themselves)

- A convention contract: *contratto convenzionati* (contains pre-determined conditions – a three-year contract with a two-year renewal option, although the initial period can be increased to five years with no renewal option. This contract can also be arranged for short-term periods, such as six months or a year; an option which suits university students and transitory workers).

As a renter with a free market or convention contract, you are reasonably secure. With a free market contract the landlord must wait till the termination of the contract before he/she reclaims the property – and only in special cases can they terminate the lease (in writing with at least six months' notice). With a convention contract, the landlord has the right to terminate the contract with six months' notice.

For three informative articles on Italian rental contracts, please visit hyperlinks 40-42 in the Resources section.

What is Residenza (Residence)?

Residence in the Italian sense is a different concept from what it is in English-speaking countries. Basically, *residenza* is a confirmation of physical residence at an address.

Why do I need it?

If you are planning to stay in Rome long-term, it is worth getting *residenza*. Without it, you cannot buy a scooter or a car, obtain an Italian driver's license or see a doctor via the public health system. Once you have *residenza*, you can also get an Italian *carta di identità* (identity card).

How do I get it?

Getting *residenza* can be a convoluted process – and the process keeps changing and evolving. At the time of writing (2013), the process for getting *residenza* in Rome is as follows:

1. EU citizens who are intending to live in Rome for longer than three months need to go to their local *Anagrafe del Municipo* (City Registry Office) and complete the Declaration of Residence (*dichiarazione di residenza*).

    • The State Police have a handy page in English, with a link to the form you have to fill out, which explains the process:
    • www.poliziadistato.it/articolo/10930/

    • To get the form (with an indecipherable translation in English) just click on the link to the PDF that says "register with the local anagrafe".

    • Virgilio has a handy list of Rome's Anagrafe offices – so find out which one is closest to you (please see hyperlink 45 in the Resources section)

    • Getting this registration done within your first few weeks in Rome will mean that you are 'in the system'. But, believe me, that's the easy part!

2. Once you have registered with the *anagrafe*, got yourself an apartment or room to rent and are working – it's time to begin the journey towards obtaining *residenza*.

    What you are after now is a *certificato di residenza* (certificate of residence). To do this you need to have a 'suitable place of residence' – which means a room or apartment with a proper tenancy contract. If this isn't possible (and often landlords get nervous if you try to get *residenza* while renting off them), you can provide a letter from the person you are subletting from, stating you are a guest – *ospite* (this option seems to satisfy the authorities).

3. Check that your local *Anagrafe* does the *"certificato di residenza"* – as some do not. You can click on the *"documenti disponibili"* (Available Documents) button (please see hyperlink 45 in the Resources section) under each listing, to check this.

Check out the opening hours for your local *Anagrafe* and queue early. Bring the following with you, plus photocopies of everything:

- completed declaration of residence (*dichiarazione di residenza*) form (see previous page) – for EU passport holders

- your *codice fiscale* (tax code) – please see Chapter Two – The Basics

- EU passport, plus three photocopies, or Non-EU passport and *Permesso di Soggiorno* (Permit of Stay) plus three photocopies

- Bank Statement from an Italian Bank account (again, please see Chapter Two – The Basics, for information on opening one of these). Your bank account has to show a minimal balance (*minimo sociale*) to prove that you have the funds to live and work in Italy – this is approximately 5,500 Euros (at the time of writing)

- health insurance – you can get this from your home country or buy it in Rome

- a copy of your rental contract or a letter from the person you are subletting from, stating that you are a guest (*ospite*)

- document of *stato civile* (marital status). This can be obtained from your country's consulate in Rome. If you are British, it is worth noting that the British Embassy issues something called an 'informative note' that states that in the UK, a central registry where it is possible to obtain a Certificate of Civil Status, does not exist. Get the embassy to print out this out for you, as it should be very helpful (please see <u>hyperlink 46 in the Resources section</u>)

- your job contract with your last pay cheque – or your *Partita IVA* (please see <u>Chapter Five – Getting a job</u>) if you are self-employed

- two *marche da bollo* (government stamps) worth 14.62 Euros each – you can purchase these from your local tobacconist's and two more *marche da bollo* worth 0.52 cents from the *Cassa Comunale* (City Council Cash Desk). You'll find this on the first floor of the *Anagrafe* on Via Petroselli

- six passport photos (uncut) that you can get done from booths all over central Rome.

Once you reach the head of the queue, hand over all your documents. If the person entering all your data is happy with everything, you will be given a "*fascia*" or print-out (valid for three months) that states you are in the process of getting *residenza*. You can use this *fascia* to sign up with your local health authority, until the actual document arrives.

Within the three-month period, a *vigile urbano* (city or municipal police officer) will pay you a visit to ensure that you actually live at the address you provided. Make sure you have your rental contract or letter stating you are a guest (see above) to hand, as he/she may ask to see it.

When your *certificato di residenza* has been completed, you will receive notification that it is ready for collection from the Anagrafe! Once you have your Residence Certificate you can now get an identity card (*carta di identità*)!

For more detail on this process, please visit hyperlinks 47-50 in the Resources section.

Apartment Living in Rome

I've always found Roman apartments comfortable to live in, and the standard of Italian building to be generally quite high. They have tiled or parquet flooring, and the thick stone walls ensure insulation and soundproofing is pretty good. Rome does not have a lot of double-glazing, and when they do it is more to reduce traffic noise than insulate. However, many buildings are centrally heated in winter (from November to the end of March). Kitchens are functional, space-saving and, generally, not fitted.

Most Italians cook with gas so expect to find either a gas hob or oven – or both. You will also find a nifty cupboard above the sink, where you drain your dishes (rather than drying them with a tea-towel). Bathrooms tend to be marble tiled, and many have bath-tubs (although you may find that small studio apartments will have shower cubicles instead).

Apartment living in Rome is a lot of fun. Provided you don't end up with the neighbours from hell, most buildings are little communities of their own. Many have a *portiere* (porter) who keeps an eye on who comes in-and-out of the building. He often sorts the mail, and holds onto parcels, for the tenants, and makes sure the entrance is kept clean and tidy. Become acquaintances with, or befriend, some of your fellow tenants, and you will soon feel like it's 'your building'.

CHAPTER FIVE – GETTING A JOB

With a few exceptions – and I will go into these – most people do not move to Rome in order to further their career. If climbing the 'career-ladder' and living for your work defines a large part of your character then Rome will frustrate the hell out of you in no time. I am not saying that Rome is a career black-hole, but it is a city where a great lifestyle vastly outweighs career prospects. As a foreigner, you are at a disadvantage, especially if you compete for jobs against Italian graduates. You will be new to the system, not a native speaker and, unless you can offer a skill that Italians cannot, you will be passed over in favour of Italian nationals – just as they would be in your home country.

With this in mind, how do you go about looking for work in Rome?

Firstly, look at what you have to offer. If you are very young, recently graduated from University or with very little work experience, and know basic Italian you will be limited to a few professions. These include:

- English Language Teaching (however, to work for a decent school you will need a university degree and or life/work experience, plus a teaching certificate)

- Tour guiding
- Bar tending
- Au-pair work

If you have a bit of life experience, and specialised skills, then your options widen. For example, if you have a strong business or legal background, you can mix this with language teaching and command a good hourly rate. If you have had experience as an administrator and you obtain CILS certification, your English skills could get you a job in an office that requires bi-lingual staff.

If you are looking for work in the private sector, and if you get CILS certification (and have marketable skills) you can try:

- Finance administrator
- Accounting technician
- Paralegal/legal secretary
- Beautician
- Hairdresser
- Real estate agent
- Sales
- Personal trainer/fitness coach

If you wish to blend your English language ability with a teaching qualification you can try:

- Qualified preschool/early childhood teacher
- English Language Teacher for a private school
- English language/Literature Teacher at University Level
- English Language Teacher at high school level.

Note: for the last two positions it is likely you will have to sit a *concorso pubblico* (public exam/competition) as part of the application process.

What is a concorso pubblico?

If you want to work for a university, public school, state-run company or for any regional, local or city council in Italy you will need to sit a *concorso pubblico*. Think of it as an interview process involving an open exam that covers a number of subjects, with a language component (these will depend on the job you are applying for).

The public examination/competition process is a long, convoluted one – and the testing is rigorous.

The *Concorsi Pubblici* website has more information on public exams and a list of the *concorsi* currently available (in Italian) in Rome:
www.concorsipubblici.com/provincia-roma.htm

Where to look for a job in Rome

Wanted in Rome and Craigslist both have job listings in English:

Wanted in Rome – jobs:
www.wantedinrome.com

Craigslist – Jobs in Rome:
www.rome.en.craigslist.it/jjj/

Portaportese and Bakeca both have extensive job listings in Italian:

Portaportese – Lavoro:
www.portaportese.it/rubriche/Lavoro/

Bakeca – Offerte di Lavoro:
www.roma.bakeca.it/offerte-di-lavoro-0

Here are a few tips for job-hunting in Rome:

- Learn Italian (yes, I've mentioned this a few times!) – get fluent and sit the CILS exams if you want to get an office or administration job. You will be competing against locals so you need your written Italian to be A1!

- Reformat your CV/Resume into Italian format. The Italian-style CV is quite straight-forward, written in chronological order and not as brief as the American-style resume. Please see Appendix 1 at the back of this book for a template.

- A good cover letter is essential, and your goals and skills go here rather than in your CV. Please see Appendix 2 at the back of this book for a template.

- Note that in Italy, many jobs are not advertised and that the personal touch is valued above all else. This means that you should decide where you would like to work and send in your Italian-formatted CV and cover letter, explaining the skills you offer and how you can help their organisation.

The Necessary Details: Contracts and Paying Tax

Employment Contracts

Under Italian law every employee must be given a *contratto di lavoro* (employment contract) and there are two types: '*dipendente*' (for employees) and contracts for apprentices or those in work-training. As a foreigner, you are likely to fall into the first category, of which there are two types:

1. Fixed term (*contratto a termine or contratto a tempo determinato)* or
2. Permanent *(contratto a tempo indeterminato*)

If you are offered a *'contratto a tempo indeterminato'* then congratulations – these contracts are highly sought after and held on to once obtained. A permanent contract gives you generous annual leave, sick leave and maternity leave (Italy's maternity leave is some of the most generous in the world). Plus, you receive a 'thirteenth month' bonus pay at the end of each year.

However, many people end up with a fixed term or temporary contract.

The *'contratto a progetto'* temporary employment contract is a short-term contract that is valid only for a 'project' or 'phases of a project'. Since this is the contract most foreigners end up with, it is worth noting its characteristics.

- Once your project contract ends, your employer can offer you the same contract, over and over again, without legally being required to offer you something permanent.

- Your employer can terminate your contract with only a month's notice, and does not need to give *'giusta causa'* (just cause) for your dismissal.

- You can use your *codice fiscale,* so no need to get a *Partita IVA* (VAT or GST number).

- Your employer will pay tax on your behalf, as well as two-thirds of the usual INPS (pension/social security) contributions (see below about registering for INPS) – you pay the other third.

- You are also protected by accident insurance (paid by your boss), and are permitted to ask for a few days 'suspension' of your contract if you have an accident or fall ill. The downside of this is that your employer could decide to terminate the contract (with at least one-month's notice).

- Women are also entitled to maternity leave (five months before and after childbirth). You are able to put your work contract on hold while you are on leave – and you are eligible to receive 80% of your total salary received in the 365 days prior to taking maternity leave.

- In addition to maternity leave, women also can take up to three months off (without risking their job) during their child's first year.

Registering for INPS

INPS (*Instituto Nazionale Previdenza Sociale*) is Italy's social security/state pension system. All those working in Italy (including EU and non-EU citizens) are eligible to sign up. INPS also handles maternity leave, and disability and unemployment benefits. However, INPS does not cover the public health system, which is a separate entity (see Chapter Two – The Basics).

Once you register for INPS, your employer will contribute on your behalf.

Rome has a few INPS offices. Visit the official site to see which one is closest to you: www.inps.it/portale/default.aspx

Make sure you check the office's opening times (*Orari di apertura al pubblico*) to save yourself a fruitless visit!

For more information on INPS and on how Italy's social security system works, please visit hyperlinks 57-58 in the Resources section.

Paying Tax

You will need a *codice fiscale* (tax code) in order to be paid legally in Italy (please see Chapter Two – The Basics). Once you get your tax code, just provide your employer with the details and they will take care of the rest.

If you decide to work freelance, you will need a *Partita IVA*.

Who needs a Partita IVA and how do I get one?

If you are self-employed (*lavoratore autonomo*) or a sole trader (*ditta individuale*), you will need to get a *Partita IVA*. This is the equivalent to a VAT or GST number, which allows you to invoice for your services and collect IVA on behalf of the state.

EU citizens residing in Italy are entitled to carry out the above types of work on a temporary or permanent basis, under the same terms as Italian citizens.

Registering for your Partita IVA is relatively straightforward and free of charge, although if your Italian is limited you will need a local or fluent speaker to translate for you. To get your Partita IVA you will need to:

1. Download the registration form (hyperlink 59 in the Resources section) and fill it in.

   You will also want to download the 'instructions for filling in the form' (hyperlink 60 in the Resources section) – *Istruzioni per la compilazione*.

   • Both the form and the instructions are in complicated Italian so you will need a good dictionary and the help of a native speaker (preferably someone who is self-employed) to decipher it. Some of the information you will be asked to provide may have you scratching your head, but (as with most official forms) often the information they are asking for is quite simple. For example, you should tick the box "Contribuenti minimi"* if your income is less than 30,000 Euros per year (this will put you in a simplified tax bracket).

* Note: From 2012, it appears that there will be changes to the 'Contribuenti Minimi' tax bracket – ask your accountant about this.

Dottore Commercialista has more information about your IVA payments (in Italian) –please see hyperlink 61 in the Resources section).

- You will also need to choose the correct code (*codice attività*) that corresponds to your job. Visit the ISTAT website and enter your type of business into the search field (e.g. *architetto* – architect – or *fotografo* – photographer).

- ISTAT also has a full list of all the job codes – please see hyperlink 62 in the Resources section.

- For a full list of all the job codes, please see hyperlink 63 in the Resources section.

- When filling in the form (*modello*) you will probably only have to complete sections A, B, C, D and F (this section asks you to provide the name and address of the person who files your IVA returns – either yourself or your accountant – *commercialista*). Sections E and G only relate to business changes.

- While on the subject of accountants – it is a good idea to find yourself a trustworthy *commercialista* (ask for recommendations from self-employed Italians). An accountant will file your IVA returns on your behalf (usually every three months) and keep your books in order. The service should not cost more than 300-800 Euros a year, so if you get a higher quote, go elsewhere!

2. Once you have filled in the form, go to the *Agenzia di Entrate* (Income Agency) in Rome – please see Chapter Two – The Basics, for the address. If you have filled in the form correctly, and provided the right code (*codice attività*) they should provide you with your IVA number on the spot!

Furthering your career in Rome

At the beginning of the chapter, I mentioned that there are exceptions to the "don't come to Italy to further your career" rule – and there are. Italy can be the land of opportunity for resourceful, creative types who have specialist skills and excellent language skills (Italian, English and another language). There are also a few foreigners living in Rome, who work as freelancers for overseas companies and are paid in British pounds or US dollars.

Big organisations such as the FAO (Food and Agriculture Organization of the United Nations) are based in Rome, and do hire specialists. The FAO is worth contacting if you have a background in biotechnology, climate change, capacity development, fisheries, forestry or agro-industries: www.fao.org

Whatever field you choose, remember that there is a recession on, and Italy has been hit hard. Life is a bit tougher these days and job hunting may take a little longer than you anticipated. However, that said, if you prepare well, present your skills to the best of your ability and remember that you came here to enjoy life, working in Rome can be great fun!

CHAPTER SIX –
TEACHING ENGLISH IN
ROME

Teaching English in Rome is a great option for native English speakers looking for work. This chapter will talk you through the different aspects of finding ESOL work in Rome; from getting started, to finding a job, and the different teaching options available. However, I would like to start off by talking a little about the job itself and the things you should take into consideration when trying out English language teaching.

I have worked as a language teacher since the age of twenty-three. With an honours degree in English Literature, teaching may have seemed the obvious option – yet, initially, I only tried it in Rome as a means of living there without having to work as an au pair or dishwasher. I was delighted to learn that ESOL suited my personality perfectly. My first reaction was: "Wow, I get paid to talk to people!" Fourteen years later, and I still love teaching. There were times, in my late twenties especially, when I took on too many lessons and suffered burn-out, and there were times when I tried office work for a change. Yet, I have always come back to teaching because it is gives me a unique combination of freedom, creativity, self-expression and personal satisfaction.

Over the years, I have observed many others who have taken up English language teaching in Rome. Many friends began teaching years ago and are still doing so. These friends have spent over a decade slowly building up a network of contacts and on-going relationships with language schools and institutions. They take a highly professional approach to teaching – it is not seen as 'a means to an end' or a crappy job to tide them over until something better turns up. As a result, they have steady work and loyal students who come back year after year. By the same token, I have met many who started teaching in Rome without any real enthusiasm for teaching or the English language. As such, I cannot overstate the following:

Teaching English is not the easy option!

If people get on your nerves, or if you lack patience and couldn't care less what the difference is between the Present Perfect Simple and Past Simple; then I would advise you to look into other job possibilities in Rome. Teaching can't be faked. It's a vocation rather than a career. I have always found that teaching takes me out of myself. I can forget about my own thoughts or worries for an hour or two as I focus on someone else; I can be more extrovert than usual, act out situations with my students, and I love seeing them develop confidence and fluency.

If you believe teaching English isn't a 'real job' then you won't last long in this field. You'll also irritate both students and colleagues as you whine on about the fact that you were earning three times this when you were living in London or about how back in Sydney you had job security. Did you really come to Rome in search of a huge pay packet and permanent contract? Surely not!

Italians are great fun to teach. Many Romans have a dry, earthy sense of humour and most of your students will be expressive, talkative and enthusiastic. The role of 'teacher' in Italian society is viewed with respect; in many cases you will be addressed as 'professore' or 'professoressa', which actually translates as 'teacher', rather than 'professor' – but still sounds impressive! To finish off this introduction, here are some characteristics that will serve you well as an English Language teacher in Rome – if I had followed all of these, I could have avoided a lot of drama and frustration over the years!

- **Enthusiasm** – this is infectious. If you genuinely find your own language interesting, and share this with your students, they will also share your passion.
- **Curiosity** – Italians are nosy, so don't be afraid to ask questions back – use these as an opportunity to practice the interrogative form!
- **Drama** – many seem to believe that only extroverts make good teachers. This is rubbish – actually, some of the best teachers I've encountered are actually quite shy. Yet, in their teaching role they become actors, captivating their students' attention and encouraging them to express themselves. Italians love drama, so don't be afraid to give them some!
- **Respect** – it's pretty ugly to witness a teacher using a conversation class or formal lesson to rant about their crappy personal life, or to get on their soap box about all the things they don't like about Rome and Italians. I'd advise you not to go there – look beyond yourself and your opinions; there is a world of things to talk about. Try to keep the tone as positive and respectful as possible.
- **Patience** – not everyone learns quickly and some students will need you to explain concepts many times, in a few different ways, before the light bulb goes on. Take a deep breath at these moments and focus on how frustrated your student is probably feeling. Believe me, they want to understand!
- **Creativity** – although you will be given course books and materials to work off, start creating as many of your own personalised materials as possible. Pop the original copy into

a folder and by the end of the year you will have a file of original material that you can refine and use again and again.
- **Balance** – your job shouldn't take over your life. Even if you discover, as I did, that you really enjoy teaching, try not to get emotionally involved in it. Don't shy away from facing your financial situation either. Try to save a little of what you earn and live within your means. If you end up teaching thirty hours a week, and travelling all over Rome to do so – you are going to end up exhausted and bitter.

So, if you are keen to teach English in Rome, here are some useful guidelines to get you started.

Qualifications and Experience

You can come to Rome with no teaching experience (I did), but you will need to get a teaching certificate before you start looking for work. There are loads of teaching qualifications out there, but they do vary in quality – if you're serious about teaching, try to do the best you can afford. A good qualification will not only make it easier to find work with Rome's more respected language schools, but will also give you a solid understanding of teaching and the confidence to stand in front of a class and explain the First Conditional without wilting!

You can get qualified before you come to Italy. Your local university will run ESOL certificates and diplomas. International House runs teacher training courses world-wide; their CELTA (Certificate of English Language Teaching to Adults) is one of the world's best: www.ihworld.com/teachers

If you have arrived in Rome without a teaching certificate, then I highly recommend doing your CELTA at International House, Rome (Viale Manzoni 22). They run between four and six one-month intensive (9am-5pm/Mon-Fri) courses per year. They also run a few semi-intensive courses that last three months (Tuesdays and Thursdays/9am-5pm). The CELTA course encourages you to work closely with other trainee teachers. You teach classes at elementary, pre-intermediate and intermediate levels, while being observed by your peers and tutor. The course also has a number of theoretical assignments due each week. For more information on the CELTA, including up-to-date information on dates and prices, visit International House, Rome's website: www.ihromamz.it/

Of course, you could try your hand at teaching without a qualification – and a few years ago many did – but these days the market is a lot more competitive. Qualified teachers with at least two-three years experience should find job hunting relatively easy. If you have no certificate and no experience you will probably end up teaching for small schools that are run on a shoestring (with poor wages to match).

If you get super serious about teaching English, and have at least five years experience under your belt, it's worth thinking about doing the Diploma of English Language Teaching to Adults (DELTA). This qualification is essential if you want to work as a Director of Studies (D.O.S) at a language school: www.ihromamz.it/delta.html

Getting started

Before you embark on teaching English in Rome, or anywhere, for that matter, there are a few essentials you shouldn't be without:

- A good English grammar reference book. I recommend: *English Grammar in Use* by Raymond Murphy (you want the intermediate book with the blue cover). This is an English language teacher's grammar bible! You can study some of the finer points of English grammar and photocopy some of the exercises, when necessary, to use with your students. For more information on this book, please see hyperlink 68 in the Resources section.

- A laptop (even a mini one) – bring it from home as it is likely to be cheaper than buying a laptop in Rome. Plus, the European keyboard takes some getting used to!

- A printer. These are pretty cheap and available from most electronics stores throughout Rome – essential for printing out lesson plans, articles from the internet and your own materials.

- Internet access – try to get this sorted early on. Having access to English news and internet resources will make lesson planning much easier. See <u>Chapter Two – The Basics</u> – the section on telephone and WiFi internet access.

- A diary – whether it is on your smart phone or tablet, or whether (like me) you prefer a printed diary, one with plenty of space to write all your lessons in is essential. When I'm teaching, I carry my whole life around in my diary, especially as private lessons can vary from week-to-week.

- A set of A4 plastic envelopes and plastic files to keep your lesson plans/materials in.

- A set of whiteboard pens, an A4 notepad, a selection of pencils and pens – and some felt tip pens, glue-stick and scissors. You should be able to buy all of these at any *cartoleria* (stationery shop) in Rome.

Looking for teaching work

As mentioned in the previous chapter, September/October and January/February are the best times of year to look for teaching work. Don't arrive in June expecting to find work over the summer (unless you contact a school looking for summer camp teachers), as work dries up from the beginning of July till mid-September.

When looking for teaching work, your first port of call should be *Wanted in Rome*. The online and printed editions both have extensive listings of teaching jobs, for teachers of all backgrounds and experience:
www.wantedinrome.com/classifieds/jobs-vacant.html

When it comes to job hunting, the methodical approach often works best. The following process has always worked for me when looking for teaching work in Rome:

1. Get your CV/Resume up-to-date. Write your CV in English (as it will be received by a native English-speaking D.O.S) Make it as 'teaching' and 'communication' focused as possible. Even if you have little, or no, teaching experience, highlight anything that makes you appear like a strong communicator. It could be the seminar you helped present at work last year, or the job training you assisted with. Also, anything that shows skill with the English language: writing, journalism, translation, editing etc. All these will impress your prospective D.O.S. It's also worth emphasising any specialist skills you may have. Do you have a degree in law, medicine or accountancy? Make sure you highlight these, as schools and companies are often on the lookout for teachers with specialist backgrounds.

2. Go through the job listings and choose at least five advertisements that best suit your skills, experience and qualifications. Write a one-page cover letter, introducing yourself and explaining your availability and what you would bring to the school. Try to keep the tone warm, relatively formal and confident, without coming across as arrogant. Make sure this letter is as grammatically perfect and error-free as possible (you are applying for a job as an English teacher, after all). Get a friend to proofread it before you send it off.

3. Apply for jobs – send a cover letter and CV (either via email or post – as the advertisement requests). Make sure you are easy to contact. You should have an Italian mobile phone number and an email address you check regularly.

4. Alternatively, you can go through a listing of English language schools in Rome (a Google search should give you a comprehensive list), pick out five that you feel would suit your skills and experience best – then email or post them a cover letter and a copy of your CV.

5. If you have no bites from the above process, repeat steps two, three (and four if you like) until someone calls you in for an interview.

6. Once you are called in for an interview, take it as seriously as you would for a job interview back home. Years ago, prospective teachers may have turned up looking rough and still got the job but these days you need a competitive edge. Dress smartly and bring a printed copy of your CV, and the original of your teaching certificate.

7. Some schools will give you a grammar test, or ask you a few questions about how you would teach certain grammar points, before hiring so it may be worth studying up on Raymond Murphy's *English Grammar in Use*, and materials from your teaching certificate course, beforehand.

8. The school may also want to see you teach a class before they hire you – they will give you a grammar point to teach and will want to see a lesson plan as well. Don't be intimidated by this – but if you are inexperienced it's better to err on the side of simplicity. Your prospective D.O.S will want to see that you can teach the basics well, using a warm, engaging teaching style, rather than anything flashy. Nerves can get to you in these situations, but the key to overcoming

it is to speak slowly, breathe deeply and ignore the person observing you!

9. If the interview goes well, you should, hopefully, be offered work. If you are lacking experience, do not be afraid to ask for higher level classes, such as Intermediate, to start off with, rather than being thrown in the deep-end with a group of beginners.

10. A good school will also be transparent about what classes they have available. When discussing/accepting work, watch out for the following:

- Vague promises from a D.O.S who expects you to keep twenty hours available a week but won't tell you where and when your lessons will be.

- Offers that will have you teaching an hour here, and another there, all over Rome, rather than a block. You should be looking for a minimum two-lesson block (1 ½ hours per lesson on average) to make it worth your while (you may have to be firm about this one, as a surprising number of schools try this on).

- Schools that don't ask to see your teaching certificate; don't get you to sign a short-term contract; or don't ask you to provide your *codice fiscale* (tax code) – see Chapter Two – The Basics, for information on getting one of these. These schools don't care who their teachers are, besides the fact that they are native speakers, and are probably intending to pay you *in nero* (literally 'in black' – 'under the table'). Your personal situation might mean that these types of schools are the only option open to you, but just be aware that you will be reliant on your new boss's honesty to hand over your money at the end of the month.

- Lack of clear instructions and direction. Your new D.O.S should provide you with all the materials, any teaching support you may need and a clear indication of what to expect from each new class (level, materials, class size, duration and frequency and any special requirements). It's not a good sign if you have to drag this information out of them.

Should I seek work with schools, or look for private work?

There are pros and cons of working for a language school versus working for yourself.

The advantage of working for a school is that all the administrative tasks, finding of students to fill classes, organising a venue, provision of materials etc. are taken care of by the school. Most schools pay between 12-20 Euros per hour (before tax) and if they are a legitimate establishment, you will be given a *contratto a progetto* (short-term contract) with all your tax and social security contributions taken care of (please see Chapter Five – Getting a job for more details on work contracts).

When working for a language school, you are likely to be paid monthly. Teachers generally keep track of the hours they have worked in a given month, fill in a time sheet and hand it in at the end of the calendar month – you are then paid around the 12-15th of the following month. Payment methods vary, although a legitimate school should pay you by cheque or bank transfer. If you are doing a lot of travelling (e.g. your school sends you all over Rome for company courses), many schools will pay for your monthly travel pass as well. The disadvantage of working for a school is that the hourly rate is often fairly low. They also dictate the hours, duration, venue and size of the class, and they probably won't have any work for you over the summer.

What about private lessons? The upside of these is the greater hourly rate (approx 20-40 Euros per hour, depending on the qualifications, skills and experience of the teacher). You can also work the lessons in to suit your schedule, and even do some lessons at home. The disadvantage of private lessons is that if you want to stay in Italy long-term and plan to have the bulk of your income from freelance work, then you will need to get yourself a partita IVA (VAT or GST number), get yourself an accountant and do things legally (as you would back home if you worked freelance). Once again, Chapter Five – Getting a job has more details on getting a partita IVA and how it works.

Many private lessons can come through the work you do for schools. For example, you may be teaching a block of courses at a company and the boss asks if you would tutor his daughter privately, or a group of administrators in the same building approach you and ask if you would teach them privately during work hours. If you choose to accept this work, be aware that the school you are working for may get very upset about this. If they find out, you are likely to lose your job.

I have found that mixing school and private lessons works best. You could potentially do quite well by going completely freelance; just make sure you get a trustworthy accountant to guide you if you take this route.

Managing your teaching

It is important to remember that teaching English is not a classic nine-to-five job.

English language schools tend to run two types of courses:

- In-house classes, that usually take place after work (from 5pm onwards) and Saturday morning
- Company classes that usually take place during work hours at private and public institutions throughout Rome.

Any private lessons are likely to be after school/work finishes, or Saturday mornings.

If you are not a night-owl, then company courses will probably suit you better. There is a bit more travel involved, as you will have a block of lessons in different locations throughout the week. If you don't mind working evenings and/or Saturday mornings, then in-house courses will suit you. I found that, initially, evening classes suited me – but that after a while I preferred to get most of my teaching done during work hours to leave my evenings and weekends free. The beauty of teaching is that every day is going to be different. You might teach a company course for three hours one morning and then have a couple of private lessons that afternoon; then, the next day have nothing until a four hour block from 5-9pm at a language school.

Once you get your first teaching job, you will enter a steep learning curve – and discover just how much more you need to learn about the craft of teaching. It is an absorbing, dynamic and rewarding profession to be part of. Often, your students will be your best teachers!

CHAPTER SEVEN – GETTING AROUND ROME

Rome is a big city, and although the centre is compact, the clogged roads, slow public transport and general chaos remind you that it was never built for cars, buses and a metro. Getting around Rome, without doing your nut and ending up with high blood pressure to boot, is an art. In the early stages of your move, it is worth giving serious thought to the different options and to which one suits you:

- by public transport (see Chapter Two: The Basics for more details on tickets, travel passes and the metro/rail network)
- by scooter or car
- by bicycle
- on foot.

Comune di Roma

By Public Transport

If you are coming from a big city like New York or London, you can probably deal with Rome's metro and bus service for longer than most. However, even the most seasoned public transport veterans soon tire of dealing with shoving crowds, packed buses and trains, long waits, lack of personal space and thieving fingers.

If you are taking it occasionally, Rome's public transport system is fine – and it's cheap. However, cramming yourself onto a packed bus day after day will soon turn you into an angry maniac unless you develop some self-protection tactics:

- be assertive but not aggressive – this means that when boarding the bus you need to make sure you are near the back or front doors (the middle doors are for disembarking) and you need to move quickly and decisively once on the bus to ensure you get a seat. In busy periods, you are better off getting a window seat on a double row, rather than one of the single seats (although more appealing), otherwise you are likely to have to give up your seat for an elderly person. Elbowing your way onto the bus and being overly aggressive will only get you shouted at.

- give up your seat to those who need it – I know that when you're tired, or in the middle of a long bus ride, it can be tempting to ignore the elderly lady who is stomping towards you. Just swallow your irritation, smile and say *"Prego, signora/signore"* or *"Signora/signore, vuole sedersi?"* Even if everyone else seems to have forgotten their manners, remember yours – it helps remind you that even crowded in like cattle, we can still retain our humanity.

- say *"permesso"* or *"devo scendere"* – if you are at the back of a crowded bus and need to get off. The first request literally means "with permission" and the second means "I must get off". They are both assertive, but still polite, ways of actually getting off at your stop!

- say *"apre le porte per favore"* if the bus driver seems to have forgotten to open the doors

- say *"Mi scusi, la fermata?"* (you may have to shout this one!) if the bus driver fails to stop at a designated or requested bus stop.

- watch out for pickpockets. Keep your valuables zipped away in pockets inside your bag, and keep your bag on your lap or in front of you at all times – and don't carry your wallet in your back pocket. There are some infamous bus lines (such as Bus 64, which travels between Termini Station and the Vatican) where pickpockets are known to operate. Keep your wits about you, observe your surroundings at all times and be aware that some pickpockets are very good at what they do – you won't even know you've been robbed until you open your bag and find your wallet missing!

- watch out for sleazes. Yes, unfortunately, there are a few of these on Roman buses. Although it is embarrassing, women should not be afraid to confront someone who is attempting to rub up against you (or to use your umbrella as a deterrent). Public shame works a treat for getting these individuals to disappear, and will encourage other passengers to support you. Avoid being abusive as this can backfire. Phrases along the lines of the following, usually work:

  "Come si permette!" – How dare you!
  "Non mi toccare!" – Don't touch me!
  "Mi da un po' di spazio!" – Give me some space!
  "Lasciami in pace!" – Leave me alone!
  "Si vergogna!" – Shame on you!

- walk whenever possible. Often, we take the bus out of laziness. In rush hour especially, it is often faster, not to mention more relaxing, to walk.

Taking public transport long-term, especially if your job requires you to travel around the city (for example, if you are a language teacher), will seriously erode your quality of life after a while. If your pulse starts to race at the sight of the approaching bus, it's time to explore other options.

By Scooter or Car

Travelling around Rome by scooter is exhilarating – and dangerous. A car is a safer option, but less convenient as you will have to find and pay for parking and will spend a bit of time stuck in traffic.

However, having your own wheels can be extremely liberating.

Providing you take care, drive defensively and grow eyes in the back of your head, travelling around Rome by scooter will remove a lot of stress from your day. To buy a scooter (or a car), or to get an Italian driver's licence you will need *residenza* (residence) – please see Chapter Four – Finding somewhere to live.

If you have a European driver's licence you should be able to get your licence converted.

Rome's Licensing Authority has a complete list of convertible licences (please see hyperlink 75 in the Resources section)

In most cases, if your licence is from outside Europe (and that includes the US, Canada, South Africa, New Zealand and Australia), you cannot convert it, and will have to get an International Driver's Licence before your departure. These are valid for one-year and will allow you to hire a car or scooter. However, once in Rome, you will have to rub shoulders with Italian teens and sit your scooter or vehicle-driving test if you want to be mobile on two or four wheels! I know – it's bad enough that you had to go through this once in your home country. You may have been driving for years but now you will have to do it all again!

It is a good idea to get your Italian scooter licence (*patentino ciclomotore*) or vehicle driver's licence (*patente B*) before buying a scooter or car, as you will need it to get insurance (*assicurazione*).

Third party insurance is compulsory in Italy and very expensive in Rome (where crash rates, damage and theft are commonplace). In Rome, the cost of insuring your scooter for a year starts from around 1,000 Euros, but a car can be triple that! Car insurance in Italy works on a tiered system where new drivers pay the most. As the years pass (accident-free of course!), the cost slowly decreases. For this reason, make sure you budget for the extra expense.

Rome's Licensing Authority is the place to go for all information (including test dates) relating to gaining your scooter or vehicle driver's licence:
www.motorizzazioneroma.it

For more information in English about obtaining an Italian drivers licence or scooter licence, please visit hyperlinks 76-78 in the Resources section.

If you would like to try out scooter-driving in Rome before buying one for yourself, you can hire one from Bici Baci. Remember to bring your passport, credit card and international driver's license (or EU licence):
www.bicibaci.com

To get more information on preparation for the theory and practical tests, traffic regulations and an overview of Italian driver's licences, visit:
www.scuolaguida.it

Online tests for various licenses are available in various languages, other than Italian, online at:
www.testpatente.it

By bicycle

A few years ago, it was uncommon to see cyclists navigating their way through Rome's streets – but of late that has changed. Providing you are careful (and although you are not obliged to wear a helmet, please do), it can be a fantastic way to get around Rome.

Rome's city council has been encouraging locals and visitors to use bicycles and have introduced the 'Bike Sharing' scheme for those living in Rome. This initiative has 'bike stations' throughout Rome's historic centre, and there are now 27 *ciclo-posteggi*, with 150 new green bicycles.

If you live and work in the centre, then Bike Sharing is an ideal solution. To sign up you just need to bring along your passport (and Permit of Stay, if you are not an EU passport holder) and your *codice fiscale* (tax code) to the ticket office of one of the following Metro A and B stations:

1. Stazione Termini
2. Lepanto
3. Piazza di Spagna
4. Anagnina
5. Ottaviano
6. Cornelia
7. Battistini
8. Ponte Mammolo
9. Eur Fermi
10. Laurentina

These ticket offices are open from 7am to 8pm (Mon-Sat) and 8am to 8pm (Sun).

It will cost you 10 Euros to sign up (5 Euros for the card and 5 Euros credit), and you will receive a 'Smart Card' – an electronic card that you will use to operate the Bike Sharing system. You can recharge your card at any of the ten stations above.

The service costs you 50 cents every half hour. You can use the bicycle for a maximum of twenty-four hours in one go. Bike Sharing is a 24-hour service and to pick up one of the bikes, you just place your card on the reader at the top of the stand next to each bike. This will release the bike and log you in to the service. After using the bike, you can return it to any bike station (not just the one you picked it up from), and do the same thing as when you picked up the bike, this will secure it in the stand.

For full details on the Bike Sharing service, plus to utilise the 'users login' (you'll receive your username and password when you buy your card), where you can view the trips you've taken, how much money you've spent and your balance, visit the Bike Sharing website (in Italian):
www.bikesharing.roma.it/

If you are not living in the historic centre, and want to use your own bike, then buying one is the best option. Make sure you buy a heavy chain and padlock (and use them!) or you can kiss your bike goodbye within 24-hours!

Porta Portese (Rome's online buy, sell and exchange website), has a listing of used bicycles:
www.portaportese.it/rubriche/Veicoli/Bici/

There is a row of bike shops in the actual Porta Portese area (the location of Rome's famous flea-market each Sunday), centred around Via Clivio Portuense.

For a listing of the shops in this area, plus handy tips on cycling in Rome, repairs, and a list of places where you can rent bikes, *Wanted in Rome* has an informative article online – please visit hyperlink 84 in the Resources section.

If you can spend a bit more (and want to pedal a bit less!) there are some nifty electric bicycles on the market. Take a look at Microbike, based in Rome – their prices start from around 990 Euros (and you don't need a *patentino* – scooter licence – to own one!): www.microbike.it

On foot

Rome is a fantastic city to walk in. If you live and work in the centre it is a great way to keep fit while really enjoying your city. Even if you don't live in the centre, take every opportunity you can to walk. You truly discover Rome as you wander through her backstreets – and you will feel smug as you stroll by bus loads of miserable commuters stuck in rush-hour traffic!

Here are some walking tips:

- wear comfortable shoes – stylish walking shoes or trainers (yes, some do exist!) will keep your feet in one piece as you traverse Rome's cobbled streets and uneven paving
- avoid carrying heavy bags on one shoulder (or you will end up with sore neck and shoulder muscles) and if you do have to carry books with you for work, wear a backpack.
- keep your wits about you crossing roads. Look both ways religiously and make sure you eyeball oncoming traffic as you step out onto a pedestrian crossing (or they may not stop!). When in doubt, cross with a group of people, or shadow a nun!
- carry a 500ml water bottle with you – and refill it at a *nasone*; one of the fire-hydrant style water fountains throughout Rome
- keep a good map with you so that if you do get lost, you can find yourself again!

CHAPTER EIGHT – DEALING WITH CULTURE SHOCK, AND INTEGRATING

In the Preface, I compare settling in Rome to embarking on a passionate love affair – one that can go seriously wrong if you:

- arrive with unrealistic expectations

- try to 'get to grips' with the city too quickly

- expect to settle in immediately, without any stress or Culture Shock or

- arrive with no Italian, and make no effort to learn any.

There has been plenty written on the phenomenon of Culture Shock. In his book 'The Five Stages of Culture Shock', Paul Pedersen describes the five phases a newcomer goes through before integration as: Honeymoon, Negotiation, Adjustment, Mastery and

Interdependence (Greenwood Press, 1995). The University of Otago (Dunedin, New Zealand) describes these stages as: Fun, Fright, Flight Fight and Fit – as shown in the following 'Settlement Curve' diagram.

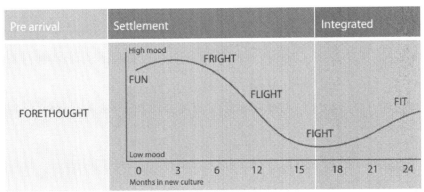

Settlement Curve Diagram (Mil Black, Relocation Manager, HR, University of Otago)

Upon moving to a new country, it is common to go through a 'curve' of emotions during the first 18-24 months. In the article that accompanies the above diagram, the author describes the 'Settlement Curve' as follows:

"After the initial high mood of arrival passes, something will happen (big or small) that causes frustration or unhappiness (Fright). If there is an absence of friends or family support at this stage, a decision to leave or return home (Flight) can occur. If support is on hand, a person can move through this period to a turning point about the reality of living here and make a conscious decision to stay (Fight). The final phase follows, and challenges become about usual everyday matters, not about being in a new country (Fit)."

It's important to understand what Culture shock is, and that it is likely to affect you, before embarking on your Roman adventure.

You arrive in Rome on a high, full of enthusiasm and excitement. Three wonderful months pass and then something happens. It could be a succession of rude shop assistants, or an unpleasant brush with Italian bureaucracy, or maybe someone knocks you off your bicycle

– whatever the trigger, it gives you a shock. You are upset that the reality isn't measuring up to your dreams; and if this upset continues over the coming months, you'll be booking your flight 'home' by the end of the year. If you knew this was coming, you could get a bit of support from colleagues and friends, and work through the frustration and the accompanying emotions (these can range from helplessness, withdrawal, irritability, boredom and homesickness, to anger, hostility towards locals, stereotypical thinking and compulsive behaviour).

After about eighteen months, things start to improve – you start to master the language and difference is accepted rather than highlighted as "Yet another reason why this country pisses me off!" You also make Italian friends and develop some of their habits. At this point, integration begins.

For more information on Culture Shock, please visit hyperlinks 86-87 in the Resources section.

Integrating in Rome

Integrating into a new culture takes time. It actually takes years to get 'under the skin' of your new home. Even if you love Italian culture (which I hope you do, since you're moving there!) and are eager to fit in and adapt to an Italian way of life, you will find that you just can't hurry integration. It seems that the younger you are, the easier it is – and maybe this is because in our teens and twenties, friendships are often more important to us than when we get older (which is a pity, as friendship is one of life's joys). At the risk of generalising, younger people tend to be a lot more mentally flexible and endure difficulties easier, such as a crappy job, or cramped living conditions. That said, most of us mellow a bit in our thirties and forties, and have more realistic expectations of life; things aren't so black and white. Because of this, there can be benefits of moving to Rome when you're older.

If there's something that living in Rome teaches you, it's patience.

So, if you are the type to start grinding your teeth when there are three people in front of you in a queue – Rome will really test you. You will need patience for everything here, from queuing in your local supermarket or post office, to mastering the language and dealing with the bureaucratic labyrinth as you attempt to get a *Permesso di Soggiorno* or *Residenza*.

You need to learn the art of patience in Rome because life moves slower. Nothing (apart from buying an espresso) is instant – and isn't that why you moved here anyway? One of my friends in Rome, who moved here from the US years ago, told me that when she gets frustrated by the city she reminds herself not to "confuse easiness with happiness". Sure, life might have been 'easier' back in the US, in terms of organisation and services, but the lifestyle – including a long, hot summer every year spent at the beach – more than makes up for it!

Even if you make friends with Romans soon after your arrival, integrating to the point where you feel you really 'fit in' takes time.

First there's the language barrier. Once you get to the point where you 'command' the language, you will really feel at home. It's a great feeling when you finally master telling (and understanding) jokes so that you can actively participate in conversations, rather than forever sitting on the outside looking in.

Second, there are the cultural differences. You are foreign, and the way you do everything, from cleaning your house and washing dishes, to bringing up your children and eating habits will be different. Of course, there will be many habits, beliefs and behaviour that you will bring with you, and should never change. They are part of who you are, and moving to a new country shouldn't mean that you leave them all behind. To do so, would be erasing part of who you are. However, observing the local social etiquette and adapting some of your habits so that you do not give offence, or constantly have to explain yourself, will make your road to integration easier.

Here are some small day-to-day things that are worth noting when it comes to 'fitting in':

- Whenever you are about to enter someone's home (and are standing on the threshold), say *"Permesso"* (with permission) before entering.

- Although you may choose to go barefoot at home – don't try this if you are a guest at someone's home. You will notice that Italians always wear slippers or flip-flops indoors if they are not wearing shoes.

- If you are doing the dishes in someone's home – remember to always rinse everything (you probably do this anyway, but just in case). Italians are very particular about this and, while we are on the subject, don't try drying dishes with a tea-towel (not considered hygienic), but stack them in the draining cupboard above the sink.

- Learn to appreciate why Italians use bidets, and don't be offended if Italians think all non-bidet-using nations are dirty; it isn't aimed at you personally!

- Always bring a little something when you go to someone's home for a meal – a bottle of wine or a little tray of pastries from your local *pasticceria* will be very appreciated.

- Italians don't order milky coffees (cappuccinos, caffè lattès or lattè macchiatos) after 11am – and they certainly don't order one after a meal (opting for an espresso or caffè macchiato instead). This is because they believe that drinking hot milk on top of a stomach full of food won't help your digestion.

- Eat bread with your starter or second (meat or fish) course – but avoid gobbling it with your first course (pasta or risotto);

otherwise, don't be surprised if you draw raised eyebrows from the Italians at the table (they are wondering how you are going to make it through the next two courses without exploding!).

There are plenty more than just the above – but remember that if you do mistakenly make some cultural faux pas, it's not the end of the world!

The road to integration can sometimes take longer than you hoped, and one destructive tendency that you should watch out for is 'hyper-sensitivity'. As you go about your day-to-day life you start to imagine locals muttering under their breaths about 'idiotic foreigners', you start to believe all Italians hate *stranieri* – foreigners (and your nationality in particular) and that your very existence in Rome offends them. I know, this sounds ridiculous (and frankly, it is) but our perceptions, wrong or right, can colour our entire world. So, if during your first year in Rome, you find yourself becoming bitchy, grumpy and paranoid – give yourself a good talking to – and remind yourself that Rome wasn't built in a day!

CHAPTER NINE –
EXPLORING ROME

So much has been written about
the glories of the Eternal City.
There are so many wonderful
books on Roman history, food,
people and culture – that to give
an overview on everything Rome
has to offer would require another
(much bigger) book, and not one
chapter! Rome's big sights, such
as the Vatican, the Coliseum, the
Trevi Fountain, the Pantheon,
Piazza Navona and the Spanish
Steps, need no introduction and
there are plenty of in-depth
guidebooks available that will
really bring these treasures to life.

However, after years spent exploring Rome and its hinterland, I
wanted to share my ten Roman favourites with you. Some of these
are just what you need when Rome's intensity starts to wear you
down (in alphabetical order):

1. Appia Antica Park

I had been in Rome for years when I finally discovered this park –
and when I did, I wondered how I had missed it! The *parco appia
antica* is enormous, and really close to the centre; stretching sixteen
kilometres of the ancient Appian Way from the Porta San Sebastiano
and the intersection with Via Appia Nuova in Frattocchie, past the
remains of seven Roman aqueducts, to the large green rural estates
of Tormarancia and Farnesiana. It is beautiful. A long ancient
cobbled road cuts through swathes of green and picturesque ruins. If
you have a bike, this will be somewhere to spend your weekends
exploring, and you can hire a *bici* for 15 Euros per day from the
Information Point (Appia Antica, 58/60).

For more information on the Appia Antica Park in English, you can
visit the official site:
www.parcoappiaantica.it/en/default.asp

2. Aventine Hill

The Aventine is a quiet oasis of green rising above the *Circo
Massimo* (where the ancient Romans used to race chariots). As you
climb the hill, surrounded by majestic umbrella pines, you pass the
Roseto di Roma Capitale (Rome's City Rose Garden) on the left (a
glorious sight from May to August). Farther up on the right, you will
find the *Giardino degli aranci* (The Orange Garden). There are a few
orange trees here, but the main reason to visit the garden is for the
incredible panorama over Rome. At the top of the hill in the *Piazza
dei Cavalieri di Malta* you will find the Priory of the Knights of
Malta. The facade and the square feature the neoclassical design of
Piranesi, the famous Italian architect and painter. Inside the priory is
a bit of an anti-climax after the exterior (although the Knights –
famous warrior monks – themselves were a fascinating order). What
brings most people here is the ancient keyhole in the Priory's heavy
wooden door. Look through the keyhole and you will see an avenue
of artfully trimmed hedges framing the Vatican's dome – a magical
sight at night!

3. Capuchin Crypt

This small crypt sits under the church of *Santa Maria della Concezione dei Cappuccini* at the beginning of Via Veneto (just outside the Metro A – Barberini stop). Some find the collection of bones inside macabre but it really is a reminder of how swiftly our lives pass. There are 4,000 bodies inside the crypt, thought to be mostly Capuchin Friars buried by the order. The crypt is made up of six tiny chapels, while the walls and ceiling are festooned in bones that have been hung in intricate patterns. As well as a crypt dedicated to the Resurrection, and the Mass Chapel, the remaining chapels are dedicated to bones: Skulls, Pelvis, Leg & Thigh Bones. However, it is the last crypt that often makes people pause and reflect: The Crypt of the Three Skeletons. The central skeleton is enclosed in an oval, symbolising life, while it holds a scythe, symbolising death. In its left hand it holds scales, symbolising the good and evil deeds judged by God. There is a sign which reads:

Noi eravamo quello che voi siete; quello che noi siamo voi sarete.
"What you are, we once were; and what we are you will become."

It's a sobering reminder and a very special place.

4. Coppedè

Coppedè is an oddly beautiful, tiny quarter of Rome well worth visiting. It was designed by Gino Coppedè, and is centred around Piazza Mincio (in the Trieste area of Rome, between Piazza Buenos Aires and Via Tagliamento). The architecture looks as if it comes from another world; a blend of ancient Greek, Roman, Baroque, Medieval and Art Nouveau. Standing in the centre of Piazza Mincio, you are surrounded by Florentine towers, Venetian palaces, mosaics, frescoes – and a sundial.

5. Ostia Antica

The ancient port of Ostia is a real treasure – and rivals Pompeii as an example of a well-preserved ancient Roman town. Best of all it is a short ride from Rome's centre. Just take the Metro B to *Piramide* and walk next door to the *Roma Porta San Paolo* train station. Take a train headed for 'Lido' – and use a regular bus or metro ticket for the journey, which should take about 45 minutes. Once you get off at 'Ostia Antica', leave the station and cross the railway bridge (which spans a busy road) and keep walking down Via della Stazione until you reach Ostia Antica's parking lot.

Ostia Antica has a wonderful, park-like atmosphere. Wander through acres of ruins surrounded by tall umbrella pines. The highlights of the ruins are the Square of the Guilds and the Baths of Neptune – both of which have fantastic mosaics.

Rick Steves has an easy to digest description on Ostia Antica, as well as a handy map:
www.ricksteves.com/plan/destinations/italy/ostia.htm

6. Piazza del Popolo

This huge square was given a makeover to celebrate Rome's 2000th birthday – turning Piazza del Popolo from a grimy traffic island, into a vast, majestic cobbled expanse that is nearly completely pedestrianised. Piazza del Popolo literally means 'The People's Square' and has a bit of an Egyptian theme going on – with an enormous obelisk in its centre and the lion fountains at its base. The square is flanked by two identical churches (*Santa Maria dei Miracoli* and *Santa Maria in Montesanto*) and sits under the shadow of the Pinco (the hill that leads into Villa Borghese). *Santa Maria del Popolo* church on the northern edge of the square is well worth a visit, especially if you are an art lover, as it has two lovely paintings by the famous Roman painter, *Caravaggio* (Crucifixion of St. Peter and Conversion on the Way to Damascus). The Piazza does have a bit of a grim history, as it was used for public executions until 1826

– but these days it's hard to imagine such violence ever took place here.

7. Porta Portese market

Every Sunday morning, from 6.30am to 2pm, Via Portuense heaves with Rome's busiest market. *Porta Portese* is an open-air flea-market that sells everything from clothes and shoes to second-hand books, paintings, furniture and knick-knacks. It has plenty of atmosphere and you are expected to barter. You can enter through the city wall (at Porta Portese itself) or, further up, from Viale Trastevere. Watch your wallet and bag as pickpockets have a field-day here!

8. San Clemente Church

I'm always wary of adding too many churches to a list of 'must see sights', as it is easy to overdose on them. However, San Clemente isn't like any other church you will ever visit. These days it's a basilica dedicated to Pope Clement I, but in reality, it is three buildings. The current basilica was built in 1100, at the height of the Middle Ages, and beneath that is the 4th century basilica. In the basement is the 2nd Century mithraeum (temple dedicated to the cult of Mithras). This was a pagan cult dedicated to the worship, and sacrifice, of the bull. The cult was particularly popular with Roman soldiers, who met in underground mithraeum and had to undergo seven steps of initiation into the cult. San Clemente is located a couple of minutes' walk from the Coliseum on Via Labicana 95.

For more information on San Clemente church, you can visit the official site (in English):
www.basilicasanclemente.com/

9. Testaccio

This grid of streets, which sits in the triangle between the Aventine Hill, the Tiber and the city walls, was once a staunchly working class district – thanks to the huge slaughterhouse (*mattatoio*) that once dominated the area. Although the slaughterhouse closed down years ago, the earthy atmosphere remains. Testaccio has a fantastic range of *trattorie* serving up rustic Roman dishes, and a great covered market.

10. Trastevere

This village-like quarter, across the river from the historic centre (Trastevere literally means 'across the Tiber'). Many foreigners end up in Trastevere's tangle of cobbled streets in the evening, as the quarter is packed full of restaurants and bars – but this area is gorgeous first thing in the morning or at sunset. The square, *Santa Maria in Trastevere* is the centre of this area. It is a wide cobbled expanse dominated by the church of the same name. Numerous bars line Piazza Santa Maria in Trastevere and it's the perfect spot to sip an *aperativo* and people watch. Other lovely squares in Trastevere are: *Piazza Sant' Egidio, Piazza Trilussa* and *Piazza San Calisto* (and the dodgy bar San Calisto – which has the cheapest drinks, and the best atmosphere, in the centre).

CONCLUSION – STAYING ON?

You've made it! Let's face it, sorting out all the practicalities of moving isn't half as fun as sitting down to a steaming bowl of *rigatoni alla carbonara* or floating on your back in the bathtub warm water of the Mediterranean – but it's essential to ensuring that your move goes smoothly, and with a minimum of stress. At the end of your first year in Rome, you want to be congratulating yourself on achieving something that most people only dream of, rather than making plans to leave. The long-term benefits of staying on in Rome are many. You can:

- have the opportunity to truly master the language (when you start dreaming in Italian you know you're there)

- look for work that utilises both your English and Italian language skills, as well as the qualifications and skills that you have brought with you

- get to build on the friendships you've made during your first year

- start to relax and enjoy settling into a Roman routine

- work towards putting roots down in your new home.

The best aspects of living in Italy: the climate, food, natural beauty, history & lifestyle – hardly need me to sing their praises. However, I do encourage you to embrace the reasons why you moved here.

Even if you are not a sun worshipper, you should experience the Italian beach holiday. Every year, Romans escape to the beach – locally to the coastline north and south of Rome, or further afield to Sardinia, Sicily or Southern Italy. The beach is not just about getting a great tan (you can spend the day sitting in the shade under your beach umbrella if you want to avoid the sun) but about relaxing. Italians spend all day at the beach, resting, reading, swimming, sunbathing and people watching. If you are a driven, super-busy person such languor will drive you mad – and that is precisely why you should experience it!

Become a student of Italian history. Learn about the rich and vibrant story of your new home and you will feel a heightened sense of connection with Rome; and a sense of how the city has evolved to its chaotic present.

Italians are passionate about food, and if you are a foodie yourself, you will fit in well here. Romans like nothing better than to discuss recipes and restaurants, and will happily teach you how to cook their favourite dishes. Become a student of Italian cuisine (I did!). You don't have to completely Italianise your eating habits (although your health will benefit if you do) but developing an Italian attitude towards food, and learning how to cook pasta as the Romans do, will definitely win you friends.

Rome and her hinterland have an endless supply of things to see and do. Lazio has always been overshadowed by its charismatic capital but it is well worth taking a blue COTRAL bus or local train out to some of the following places:

- the gorgeous villas at Tivoli – Villa Adriano and Villa d'Este

- Subiaco – a little town lost in time in the foothills of the mountains east of Rome, and the home of the San Benedictine order

- the Castelli Romani – these Roman Castles are the hill towns just south of Rome; famous for rough white wine and mouth-watering *porchetta*!

- Tarquinia – students of history will love the Etruscan museum and the necropolis (burial ground) this lovely town boasts

- the beach resorts of Ostia, Santa Marinella and Sperlonga – all easily reached by public transport

- Bracciano and Anguillara – on the shores of Lake Bracciano north of Rome.

These day-trips are also a wonderful antidote when Rome's rush and crush all gets too much for you. Rome is fantastic, but intense. You need to take the city slowly, give yourself time to settle in and take part in the daily rhythm – from that morning *cappuccino* and *cornetto* standing up at your local bar, to a lazy glass of *prosecco* as you take an *aperativo* on a Saturday afternoon and people-watch.

Moving to Rome is a great adventure, but it does come with a warning – once you make it your home, everywhere else seems a little bland, a little mundane.

Let Roma into your heart, and it will be the beginning of a love affair that lasts a lifetime.

APPENDIX 1

Here is an example of an Italian CURRICULUM VITAE. For our purposes, I have created the fictional character of Bob Bean (Note: If you are applying for an English Teaching position, your CV and cover letter will be in English).

CIRRICULUM VITAE

Nome e cognome	Bob Bean
Luogo e data di nascita	Londra, 15 agosto 1979
Residenza	1 Bond Street Londra W1, Gran Bretagna
Telefono abitazione	+44 (0) 207 111111
Telefono cellulare	+44 775 22222
Indirizzo di posta elettronica	bobbean@hotmail.com
Stato civile	Celibe (this means single, for men. Single women would put *nubile* and if you're married put *coniugato/a*)
Nazionalità	Britannica
FORMAZIONE	'A Levels' (equivalente al diploma di scuola secondaria superiore) in italiano, storia e storia dell'arte, presso il Fulham Sixth Form College.
ESPERIENZE LAVORATIVE dal dicembre 2005	Impiego presso l'ufficio postale di Regent Street, Londra.
1998-2005	Impiego presso un'agenzia di viaggio a Bond Street, Londra.
Conoscenze linguistiche	Inglese madrelingua – Italiano buono parlato e scritto
Conoscenze informatiche	Buone conoscenze. Esperienza di Microsoft Word
Interessi	La cucina, cinema, viaggio

Source: Adapted from Pocket Oxford Italian Dictionary, 4th Edition, 2010, pg 62.

APPENDIX 2

Here is an example of an Italian COVER LETTER. For our purposes, Bob Bean is applying for a job as a research assistant – *assistente ricercatore*. Note the different format to English-style cover letters. Only the date sits on the right, whereas the sender's name and address sits at the bottom of the letter. '*Oggetto*' means 'subject' and put the job reference and where you found the advert (e.g. the local newspaper). When you are writing to someone you don't know (Dear Sir or Madam) write '*Gentili Signori*'. If you are writing to a company put '*Spett.le Ditta*'.

Londra, 1 settembre 2012

Zippa Ricerca
Via Nazionale 12
10000 Roma

Oggetto: assistente ricercatore
Rif: 45433
Corriere della Sera 20.08.12

Gentili Signori

Ho letto con molto interesse il Vostro annuncio apparso sul Corriere della Sera del 20 agosto scorso e Vi sarei grato se poteste inviarmi ulteriori informazioni riguardo la posizione in oggetto.

Attualmente sono impiegato presso l'ufficio postale centrale di londra ma il mio contratto termina alle fine del mese e vorrei approfittare di questa opportunità per lavorare a Roma. Come risulta del curriculum vitae che allego alla presente, ho un'ottima conoscenza della lingua italiana.

Resto a disposizione per un eventuale colloquio nel momento che riterrete più opportuno. Dal 5 settembre di quest'anno, sarò presente a roma al seguente indirizzo:

Via Tagliamento 55
100000 Roma
Cell: 0333 33333

In attesa di un Vostro cortese riscontro porgo cordiali saluti.

Bob Bean
1 Bond Street
London W1
UK

Source: Adapted from Pocket Oxford Italian Dictionary, 4th Edition, 2010, pg 60.

RESOURCES

AUTHOR'S NOTE:

Prices go up (and sometimes, down), and information and websites change. As such, although every effort has been made to ensure all these resources are up-to-date, please feel free to get in contact with me at: samantha@romeforbeginners.com if you notice something needs updating, or if you have any suggestions or feedback.

GENERAL INFORMATION ON ROME

Read more about life in Rome from two very different expat perspectives:

As the Romans Do – by Alan Epstein
www.amazon.com/As-Romans-Do-American-Familys/dp/006093395X [1]

When in Rome – by Penelope Green
www.amazon.com/When-In-Rome-Chasing-Dolce/dp/0733619037 [2]

If you want an entertaining overview on Rome's history – without getting too bogged down by it, try reading:

Rome – by Robert Hughes
www.amazon.com/Rome-Cultural-Visual-Personal-History/dp/0307268446/ref=sr_1_1?s=books&ie=UTF8&qid=1341784050&sr=1-1&keywords=rome [3]

Lonely Planet has an excellent introduction to the sights and experiences of Rome: www.lonelyplanet.com/experiments/rome/ [4]

The Expat Guide to Rome has listings of handy practical information: www.wantedworldwide.net/browse-our-publications-online [5]

Expats Living in Rome has a wealth of information for newcomers – from language lessons, to accommodation, social events and valuable info on 'getting legal': www.expatslivinginrome.com/ [6]

ONLINE NEWSPAPERS:

Rome's newspapers:

La Repubblica
www.repubblica.it/ [7]

Il Messaggero
www.ilmessaggero.it/ [8]

FINDING SHORT-TERM ACCOMMODATION IN ROME:

Venere:
www.venere.com [9]

Wanted in Rome:
www.wantedinrome.com/ [10]

VISAS:

Find out if you need a visa to gain entry to Italy (there are some nationalities that, due to political reasons, require a visa to enter Italy): www.esteri.it/visti/home_eng.asp [11]

A list of the different types of visas for residing in Italy:
www.esteri.it/visti/tipologie_eng.asp [12]

Italy's Ministry of the Exterior has general visa guidelines that should point you in the right direction:
www.esteri.it/visti/index_eng.asp [13]

Take a look at the Anglo Info website for an overview on residency (and the various permits) in Italy:
http://rome.angloinfo.com/information/moving/residency/ [14]

ARRIVAL – TRAVELLING INTO ROME FROM FIUMICINO AND CIAMPINO

The following link provides information on the Leonardo Express and the Metropolitan Train from Fiumicino to Rome:
www.trenitalia.com/cms/v/index.jsp?vgnextoid=99eb7bd0cfdea110VgnVCM1000003f16f90aRCRD [15]

Here is a link to Terravision (for Ciampino):
www.terravision.eu/rome_ciampino.html [16]

GETTING AROUND ROME: MAPS

The Mappery has a good map of central Rome to get you started:
www.mappery.com/Rome-Tourist-Map [17]

Tuttocittà is Rome's A to Z:
www.tuttocitta.it/mappa/roma [18]

ROME'S PUBLIC TRANSPORT NETWORK:

A link to ATAC, Rome's public transport provider:
www.atac.roma.it/index.asp?lingua=ENG [19]

AGENZIA DELLE ENTRATE (INCOME AGENCY) – GETTING YOUR CODICE FISCALE

This link gives you the addresses of Rome's *Agenzia delle Entrate,* Income Agencies:
www1.agenziaentrate.it/indirizzi/agenzia/uffici_locali/lista.htm?m=2 &pr=RM [20]

PERMIT OF STAY

There are couple of handy blogs to help guide you through the Permit of Stay process:
www.escapefromamerica.com/2011/01/how-to-get-a-permit-to-stay-in-italy/ [21]
www.worldcitizeninrome.blogspot.co.nz/2011/03/labyrinth-immigration-italia-permesso.html [22]

TELEPHONES & INTERNET

Take a look at this informative blog for detailed information on this service, how to access it, and a map of free WiFi hotspots in Rome:
www.unamericanaaroma.com/2012/02/09/free-wi-fi-hotspots-in-rome/ [23]

HEALTHCARE IN ROME

European Commission's website has detailed information on the S1 form and the EHIC (for European Union residents):
www.ec.europa.eu/social/main.jsp?catId=857&intPageId=980&langId=en [24]

GETTING A POSTPAY CARD WITH THE POST OFFICE

Link to the Postpay page of Poste Italiane's website (in Italian):
www.poste.it/bancoposta/cartedipagamento/carte_postepay.html [25]

GETTING A BANK ACCOUNT SET UP WITH THE POST OFFICE

Link to the Bancoposta page of Poste Italiane's website (in Italian): www.poste.it/bancoposta/contoecarte/index.html [26]

PAYPAL

A great tool for sending money overseas, cheaply, safely and quickly:
www.paypal.com [27]
www.paypal.it [28]

LEARNING ITALIAN IN ROME:

Rome has plenty of Italian language schools. Here is a short list (though not exhaustive):

DILIT – International House:
www.dilit.it/ [29]

Torre di Babele – Italian Language School:
www.torredibabele.com/ [30]

Scuola Leonardo Da Vinci:
www.scuolaleonardo.com/Italian-language-school-Rome.html [31]

Istituto Dante Alighieri:
www.languageinitaly.com/EN/dante_alighieri.php [32]

GETTING YOUR ITALIAN LANGUAGE SKILLS CERTIFIED:

Information on CILS (Certificazione di Italiano come Lingua Straniera):
www.torredibabele.com/en/Italian_Language_Courses/CILS_Exam_and_Preparatory_Courses.html [33]

ITALIAN LANGUAGE STUDY MATERIALS

Come si dice... by Elisa Ferri and Maria Cristina Peccianti (Giunti Demetra) is an excellent self-study book that highlights communicative, everyday language, and handy situation-specific vocabulary, such as opening a bank account, registering with your local *anagrafe* (registry office), getting a *permesso di soggiorno* or applying for *residenza*. While this isn't a beginner's book, it's great once you've got a bit of elementary Italian under your belt - you can buy *Come si dice...?* on Amazon: www.amazon.it/Come-si-dice-Scuola-italiano/dp/8844035871/ref=sr_1_9?ie=UTF8&qid=1344121655&sr=8-9 [34]

ITALIAN TV

One of my favourite travel and documentary programmes is Alle Falde del Kilimangiaro:
www.allefaldedelkilimangiaro.rai.it [35]

ACCOMMODATION IN ROME:

Accommodation Listings:
www.wantedinrome.com/clas/index.php [36]
www.portaportese.it/rubriche/Immobiliare/Affitto_-_Subaffitto/ [37]
http://rome.en.craigslist.it/ [38]
www.roma.bakeca.it/case-0 [39]

Here are three articles which give more detailed information on Italian rental contracts:
http://rome.angloinfo.com/information/housing/ [40]
www.theitalywiki.com/index.php/Renting_Property [41]
www.justlanded.com/english/Italy/Italy-Guide/Housing-Rentals/Rental-Contracts [42]

For a full listing of all of Rome's suburbs, and detailed descriptions of each – Wanted in Rome has a useful "Where to live" page: www.wantedinrome.com/where-to-live [43]

RESIDENCE – RESIDENZA

The State Police have a handy page in English, with a link to the form you have to fill out, which explains the process of registering with your local *Anagrafe* upon arrival in Rome: www.poliziadistato.it/articolo/10930/ [44]

Virgilio has a handy list of Rome's *Anagrafe* offices – so find out which one is closest to you: www.roma.virgilio.it/pubblicautilita/ANAGRAFE.html [45]

If you are British, it is worth noting that the British Embassy issues something called an 'informative note' that states that in the UK, a central registry where it is possible to obtain a Certificate of Civil Status, does not exist. Get the embassy to print out this out for you, as it should be very helpful: www.ukinitaly.fco.gov.uk/en/help-for-british-nationals/living-in-italy/informative-notes [46]

For more detail on the *Residenza* process, please visit the following helpful sites:

Just Landed – Residence Permits: www.justlanded.com/english/Italy/Italy-Guide/Visas-Permits/Residence-Permits [47]

Expats Living in Rome – Getting Legal: www.expatslivinginrome.com/GETTING-LEGAL.html [48]

Anglo Info – Italian Residency: http://rome.angloinfo.com/information/moving/residency/ [49]

Polizia dello Stato (State Police) – Residency for EU Citizens:
www.poliziadistato.it/articolo/10930/ [50]

JOBS – PUBLIC EXAMS (CONCORSI PUBBLICI)

The *Concorsi Pubblici* website has more information on public
exams and a list of the *concorsi* currently available (in Italian) in
Rome:
www.concorsipubblici.com/provincia-roma.htm [51]

JOBS IN ROME – LISTINGS

Wanted in Rome and Craigslist both have job listings in English:
www.wantedinrome.com/ [52]
www.rome.en.craigslist.it/ [53]

Portaportese and Bakeca both have extensive job listings in Italian:
www.portaportese.it/rubriche/Lavoro/ [54]
www.roma.bakeca.it/offerte-di-lavoro-0 [55]

REGISTERING FOR INPS (SOCIAL SECURITY)

Rome has a few INPS offices. Visit the official site to see which one
is closest to you:
www.inps.it/portale/default.aspx [56]

For more information on INPS and on how Italy's social security
system works, please visit:
http://rome.angloinfo.com/information/money/social-security/ [57] (in
English)
www.inps.it [58] (the official site, in Italian)

REGISTERING FOR A PARTITA IVA

The Partita IVA application form:
www1.agenziaentrate.it/modulistica/altri/aa9modc_new.pdf [59] (PDF
41.4 KB)

Partita IVA 'instructions for filling in the form' (Istruzioni per la compilazione):
www1.agenziaentrate.it/modulistica/altri/aa9istrc_new.pdf [60] (PDF 68.7 KB)

For more information about your IVA payments, visit the following site (in Italian):
www.dottorecommercialista.eu/milano/regime-contribuenti-minimi.html [61]

For help choosing the correct code (*codice attività*) that corresponds to your job. Visit the following link and enter your type of business into the search field (e.g. architetto – architect – or fotografo – photographer):
http://www3.istat.it/strumenti/definizioni/ateco/atecoactr.php?testoin=architetto&invia=Cerca [62]

For a full list of all the job codes, please visit the following page:
http://www.istat.it/strumenti/defini.../STRUTTURA.zip [63]

FAO (Food and Agriculture Organization of the United Nations)

The FAO is worth contacting if you have a background in biotechnology, climate change, capacity development, fisheries, forestry or agro-industries:
www.fao.org/ [64]

TEACHING ENGLISH IN ROME

International House runs teacher training courses world-wide; their CELTA (Certificate of English Language Teaching to Adults) is one of the world's best:
www.ihworld.com/teachers [65]

International House, Rome's website:
www.ihromamz.it/ [66]

Information on the Diploma of English Language Teaching to Adults (DELTA): www.ihromamz.it/delta.html [67]

English Grammar in Use by Raymond Murphy: www.amazon.com/English-Grammar-Use-Answers-Intermediate/dp/0521532892 [68]

Wanted in Rome. The online and printed editions both have extensive listings of teaching jobs, for teachers of all backgrounds and experience: www.wantedinrome.com/classifieds/jobs-vacant.html [69]

INFORMATION ON CONTRACTS AND WORKING IN ITALY

Here are some helpful links on Italian work contracts:

www.it.wikipedia.org/wiki/Contratto_a_progetto [70]

www.ilsole24ore.com/art/SoleOnLine4/Speciali/2006/legge_biagi/tip_contrattuali_contratto_a_progetto.shtml?uuid=35329524-0e6c-11db-a453-00000e25108c [71]

www.arealavoro.org/contratti-a-progetto.htm [72]

http://italy.angloinfo.com/working/employment/types-of-job-contract/ [73]

http://rome.angloinfo.com/information/working/ [74]

GETTING AN ITALIAN DRIVERS LICENCE

Here is a link to Rome's Licensing Authority, which has a complete list of convertible licences: www.motorizzazioneroma.it/sportcond10.php [75]

Information in English about obtaining an Italian drivers licence: http://rome.angloinfo.com/information/transport/driving-licences/getting-a-licence/ [76]

Here is a blog that gives you some background information on getting an Italian driver's licence, from a foreigner's perspective: www.worldcitizeninrome.blogspot.co.nz/2011/03/getting-italian-drivers-licence-in-rome.html [77]

And here is a fun article on a South African national getting a scooter licence: www.transitionsabroad.com/listings/living/articles/getting-a-scooter-license-in-italy.shtml [78]

If you would like to try out scooter-driving in Rome before buying one for yourself, you can hire one from Bici Baci. Remember to bring your passport, credit card and international driver's license (or EU licence): www.bicibaci.com [79]

To get more information on preparation for the theory and practical tests, traffic regulations and an overview of Italian driver's licences, visit: www.scuolaguida.it [80]

Online tests for various licenses are available in various languages, other than Italian, online at: www.testpatente.it [81]

BIKING AROUND ROME

Information on Bikesharing: www.bikesharing.roma.it/ [82]

Porta Portese (Rome's online buy, sell and exchange website), has a listing of used bicycles: www.portaportese.it/rubriche/Veicoli/Bici/ [83]

For a listing of the shops in this area, plus handy tips on cycling in Rome, repairs, and a list of places where you can rent bikes, please read the following article from Wanted in Rome:
www.wantedinrome.com/articles/complete_articles.php?id_art=822
[84]

Take a look at Microbike, based in Rome – their prices start from around 990 Euros (and you don't need a *patentino* – scooter licence – to own one!):
www.microbike.it [85]

CULTURE SHOCK

Wikipedia has a succinct definition of Culture shock, as well as some common symptoms:
www.en.wikipedia.org/wiki/Culture_shock [86]

The Culture Shock series has also published a book on Rome:
www.amazon.com/Rome-Your-Door-Culture-Shock/dp/1558683062
[87]

EXPLORING ROME

For more information on the *Appia Antica* Park in English, you can visit the official site:
www.parcoappiaantica.it/en/default.asp [88]

Rick Steves has an easy to digest description on *Ostia Antica*, as well as a handy map:
www.ricksteves.com/plan/destinations/italy/ostia.htm [89]

For more information on *San Clemente* church, you can visit the official site (in English):
www.basilicasanclemente.com/ [90]

ABOUT THE AUTHOR

Samantha Charlton moved to Rome in 1998, and has spent a large part of the last decade living and working in the Eternal City. In Rome, she has lived in the areas of Ponte Lungo, Piazza Bologna and Trastevere – she also spent two years living in Spoleto, Umbria. Sam has worked as an English and Italian language tutor, translator, administrator, Italian cooking teacher and writer.

Contact Samantha at: samantha@romeforbeginners.com

www.romeforbeginners.com

If you have found this book useful, please leave an honest review on www.amazon.com so that others can find it – thank you!

Made in the USA
Lexington, KY
01 June 2013